a custom publication

Reading and Writing on the Edge
University of Massachusetts, Amherst

PEARSON

Cover Art: "Gigantia Mountains & Sea of Cortes," by R.G.K. Photography, Copyright © Tony Stone Images; "Dime," courtesy of the Shaw Collection; "Open Book On Table Edge w/Pencil," courtesy of PhotoAlto Photography/Veer Incorporated; "Open Book On Table Near Table's Corner," courtesy of Fancy Photography/Veer Incorporated; "Scrabble Pieces and a Die," by G. Herbst, courtesy of PlainPicture Photography/Veer Incorporated; "Binary codes in bowls," by John Still, courtesy of Photographer's Choice/Getty Images; "Close-up of an open book," courtesy of Glowimages/Getty Images; "College Students Sitting At Tables," courtesy of Blend/PunchStock; "Red and blue circles," courtesy of Corbis Images; "Laptop screen showing photograph of landscape," courtesy of Martin Holtcamp/Getty Images; "Apples flying," courtesy of Arne Morgenstern/Getty Images; "Riverdance," by Angela Sciaraffa; "Stone path leading through a garden" and "Book pages" courtesy of Getty Images, Inc; "Chicago" by Kristen Kiley. Additional images courtesy of Photodisc/Getty Images and Pearson Learning Solutions.

Please visit our website at *www.pearsonlearningsolutions.com*.

Attention bookstores: For permission to return any unsold stock, contact us at *pe-uscustomreturns@pearson.com*.

Pearson Learning Solutions, 501 Boylston Street, Suite 900, Boston, MA 02116
A Pearson Education Company
www.pearsoned.com

Printed in the United States of America.
VOUD

ISBN 10: 1-269-26572-5
ISBN 13: 978-1-269-26572-0

General Editors

Janice Neuleib
Illinois State University

Kathleen Shine Cain
Merrimack College

Stephen Ruffus
Salt Lake Community College

Table of Contents

Mercury Reader

Reading and Writing On the Edge

Deirdre Vinyard
University of Massachusetts, Amherst

and the

UMass Amherst Basic Writing Collaborative

Selection of Readings:

Andrea Lawlor
Liane Malinowski
Peggy Woods

Curriculum Development:

Deirdre Vinyard
Liane Malinowski

Acknowledgements

In 1989, Anne Herrington and Marcia Curtis launched the *Basic Writing* program at the University of Massachusetts, Amherst, based on the idea that students in a basic writing course need extensive practice in reading and writing, activities central to the university experience. They further recognized that these students need to engage in the type of "reader-based" writing that would be expected of them in first year composition and beyond. And they also based their curriculum on the idea that students need to be immersed in readings that speak to them—to who they are. With these principles in place, Curtis and Herrington created a theme-based reading and writing course, where students read deeply on issues of diversity and wrote with and to these texts, bringing their own personal experience and knowledge into conversation with academic texts. The first textbook for the course, created by Marcia Curtis and a group of dedicated graduate student teachers, explored themes of identity and diversity and invited students to engage with writers such as Amy Tan, Oliver Sacks, and June Jordan. Three versions of this reader, *The Composition of Ourselves*, were in use from 1994-2007.

In 2008, the program launched a new reader that I worked to create with another very dedicated group of graduate student teachers. *Reading Multiple Literacies* was used from 2008-2011. We completed a slight revision, *Engaging Literacies*, in 2011.

This new collection represents the latest version of the *Basic Writing* reader, bringing an entirely new context to the course while maintaining its basic foundation as originally conceived. In *Basic Writing* classes at UMass, students still read challenging texts on the general topic of diversity and engage those texts in their writing in a process-based writing class with a rhetorical focus. We are indebted to the vision that the founders of the *Basic Writing* course put in place.

I would like to acknowledge the small team of teachers who met over the period of two semesters to select this new group of readings. Andrea Lawlor, Liane Malinowski, and Peggy Woods volunteered to meet every Friday afternoon, despite the threat of snow storms and the lure of spring weather, to select these fresh reading choices. Each member of the committee brought a different lens to the project, making our work enlightening as well as productive. I am grateful to each member for the dedication shown to this project.

In addition, Liane Malinowski has toiled two summers, helping me to create the goals and objectives for the course and the writing prompts for each unit. Her enthusiasm for this important curricular work has been constant. I am deeply appreciative.

Deirdre Vinyard
Deputy Director, Writing Program
May 2013

Book Title: ***Reading and Writing on the Edge***

Introduction

Borders. Fences. Lines of division. Lines of definition.

Borders help define who we are. And who we are not. Borders can be visible, such as state or national borders. But many borders can be invisible. Borders mark difference and in this sense we are facing, crossing and considering borders in every part of our lives. Borders seem to be in our consciousness now more than ever.

In some ways the borders in our lives are becoming more distinct, as discussed in some of the readings to follow. Issues of immigration make us acutely aware of our national borders and the ways that these borders serve to distinguish and separate us from our geographical neighbors. In other ways we find that borders are blurry and blurring; issues of language, identity, and sometimes even space are not as clearly defined as they might seem. As a nation, the U.S. is becoming increasingly diverse and interconnected, with racial and cultural lines becoming less distinct. Too, the languages we use to communicate in an increasingly diverse country are becoming more and more varied. And so much of our interaction now happens online, erasing boundaries of distance but creating barriers of access.

This reader will guide you through an exploration of the idea of borders and borderlands. Together we will read in depth about issues of boundaries and separation and how these relate to questions of geography, identity and language. In class we will discuss these issues, reflecting on what speaks to our own experiences and what is new and different. In our writing, we will write to and with these texts, always drawing on our own knowledge of what it means to be inside, outside, or even lodged in a border.

The Course:

This text provides the reading for the *Basic Writing* course at the University of Massachusetts, Amherst. While focused on composition, this course approaches writing as an activity deeply connected to reading. And this curriculum also recognizes that to learn to read and write in meaningful and purposeful ways, we need to read and write about content that is personally and academically engaging. Therefore, this course focuses on borders as a central theme, with each chapter exploring this topic from a different angle. This approach allows us to engage deeply with many facets of one issue over an entire semester, each unit adding more insight and knowledge about it to our reading and writing.

***Readings*:**

The bulk of the readings for this class are contained in this book. A few additional readings are accessible through your classroom management system. All of these readings offer a place to engage in meaningful ways with content through active reading strategies, discussion, and exploratory writing exercises. Throughout the semester, these readings will help develop the ability to read critically and to develop a broad vocabulary on the issues presented in these texts.

***Writing*:**

A major focus of this course is writing. Along with the readings, we will engage in various generative and exploratory writing, leading to a polished essay at the end of each unit. In each unit we will read to expand ideas of the particular content area introduced, produce drafts, discuss writing with the class, revise substantially and finally copy-edit the final draft.

***Discussion*:**

An important focus of this course is class discussion, revolving around the content areas in the book and writing issues covered in class. Together we will explore the texts we read, our relationships to those texts, and the ways that we can use our interactions with these essays to create, in writing, new understandings of the way borders operate in the world.

This course will engage us in a wide variety of rich, language activities. We believe that a holistic approach to language and writing will enable the development of academic writing ability while exploring concepts about literacy that are key to the understanding of how language works. Our hope is that from this class, we will take not only a keener sense of writing, but also a critical eye to these important issues of identity in our society.

Deirdre Vinyard
Writing Program, University of Massachusetts, Amherst
May 2013

Unit 1

Unit 1 Colliding Spaces

We often imagine a border as a boundary to a physical space. But we can apply the concept of a border to non-tangible spaces as well as concrete spaces. In this unit, we will read about spatial and geographical borders through a number of different lenses, from the invisible borders of the online world, to borders in our cities that mark space and class, to the borderless, nationless world of the airport. From these readings, we will begin to construct new meanings for the word "border," and to reflect on how borders operate in our lives.

Can You Be Educated from a Distance?

James Barszcz

James Barszcz (1955–) was educated at Indiana University and Rutgers University, where he received a Ph.D. in English in 1988. He taught at Rutgers from 1980–1995. Currently, he works for AT&T as a product manager for e-mail security and lives in New Jersey with his wife and two children. He has published articles, for example, "The Cape Cod Modernism of John Peale Bishop" (2004), dealing with literature. In 2003 he delivered a paper at the American Literature Association Conference titled "Renegade Voices in Hawthorne's Letters." In 1998 he gave a talk at the AT&T User Experience Symposium titled "Help Content as Poetry," and in 1996 "Getting Lost in Gopher Space" appeared as a feature article in the AT&T WorldNet Service at Home Web site. In the following selection, Barszcz asks whether distance education can provide what he calls a "true education."

1 By almost any measure, there is a boom in Internet-based 1
instruction. In just a few years, thirty-four percent of American colleges and universities have begun offering some form of what's called "distance learning" (DL), and among the larger schools, it's closer to ninety percent. If you doubt the popularity of the trend, you probably haven't heard of the University of Phoenix. It grants degrees entirely on the basis of online instruction. It enrolls 90,000 students, a statistic used to support its claim to be the largest private university in the country.

While the kinds of instruction offered in these programs will differ, DL usually signifies a course in which the instructors post syllabi, reading assignments, and schedules on websites, and students send in their written assignments by e-mail. Other forms of communication often come into play, such as threaded messaging, which allows for posting questions and comments that are publicly viewable, as a bulletin board would, as well as chat rooms for real-time interchanges. Generally speaking, face-to-face communication with an instructor is minimized or eliminated altogether.

The attraction for students might at first seem obvious. Primarily, there's the convenience promised by courses on the Net: you can do the work, as they say, in your pajamas. But figures indicate that the reduced effort results in a reduced commitment to the course. While the attrition rate for all freshmen at American universities is around twenty percent, the rate for online students is thirty-five percent. Students themselves seem to understand the weaknesses inherent in the setup. In a survey conducted for eCornell, the DL division of Cornell University, less than a third of the respondents expected the quality of the online course to be as good as the classroom course.

Clearly, from the schools' perspective, there's a lot of money to be saved. Although some of the more ambitious programs require new investments in servers and networks to support collaborative software, most DL courses can run on existing or minimally upgraded systems. The more students who enroll in a course but don't come to campus, the more the school saves on keeping the lights on in the classrooms, paying custodians, and maintaining parking lots. And, while there's evidence that instructors must work harder to run a DL course for a variety of reasons, they won't be paid any more, and might well be paid less.

5 But as a rule, those who champion distance learning don't base 5
their arguments on convenience or cost savings. More often, they claim DL signals an advance in the effectiveness of education. Consider the vigorous case made by Fairleigh Dickinson University (FDU), in Madison, New Jersey, where students—regardless of their expectations or desires—are now required to take one DL course per year. By setting this requirement, FDU claims that it recognizes the Internet as "a premier learning tool" of the current technological age. Skill in using online resources "prepares our students, more than others, for life-long learning—for their jobs, their careers, and their personal growth."

Moreover, Internet-based courses will connect FDU students to a "global virtual faculty," a group of "world-class scholars, experts, artists, politicians, and business leaders around the world."

Sounds pretty good. But do the claims make much sense? First, it should be noted that students today and in the future might well use the Internet with at least as much facility as the faculty. It's not at all clear that they need to be taught such skills. More to the point, how much time and effort do you suppose "world-class scholars" (much less politicians and business leaders) will expend for the benefit of students they never meet or even see? Probably a lot less than they're devoting to the books, journal articles, and position papers that are already available to anyone with access to a library.

Another justification comes from those who see distance learning as the next step in society's progress toward meritocracy. A recent article in *Forbes* magazine cites Professor Roger Schank of Northwestern University, who predicts that soon "students will be able to shop around, taking a course from any institution that offers a good one. . . . Quality education will be available to all. Students will learn what they want to learn rather than what some faculty committee decided was the best practical compromise." In sum, says Professor Schank, who is also chairman of a distance-learning enterprise called CognitiveArts, "Education will be measured by what you know rather than by whose name appears on your diploma."

Statements like these assume education consists in acquiring information ("what you know"). Accept that and it's hard to disagree with the conclusions. After all, what does it matter how, or through what medium, you get the information? But few truly educated people hold such a mechanistic view. Indeed, traditionally, education was aimed at cultivating intellectual and moral values, and the "information" you picked up was decidedly secondary. It was commonplace for those giving commencement speeches to note that, based on etymology, education is a drawing out, not a putting in. That is, a true education *educes,* or draws out, from within a person qualities of intellect and character that would otherwise have remained hidden or dormant.

Exactly how this kind of educing happens is hard to pin down. Only in part does it come from watching professors in the classroom present material and respond to student questions, the elements of education that can be translated to the Net with reasonable fidelity. Other educational experiences include things like watching how professors joke with each other (or not!) in the hallways, seeing what kinds of pictures are framed in a professor's office, or going out for coffee after class with people in your dorm. Such experiences, and countless others, are sometimes labeled (and dismissed) as "social life on campus." But they also contribute invaluably to education. Through them, you learn a style, in the noblest sense of that term, a way of regarding the information you acquire and the society you find yourself in. This is what the philosopher Alfred North Whitehead meant when he called style the ultimate acquisition of a cultivated mind. And it's the mysterious ways of cultivating that style that the poet Robert Frost had in mind when he said that all that a college education requires is that you "hang around until you catch on." Hang around campus, that is, not lurk on the Net.

The Death and Life of Great American Cities

Jane Jacobs (1961)

from Chapter 2: "The Uses of Sidewalks: Safety."

...A city sidewalk by itself is nothing. It is an abstraction. It means something only in conjunction with the buildings and other uses that border it, or border other sidewalks very near it. The same might be said of streets, in the sense that they serve other purposes besides carrying wheeled traffic in their middles. Streets and their sidewalks, the main public places of a city, are its most vital organs. Think of a city and what comes to mind? Its streets. If a city's streets look interesting, the city looks interesting; if they look dull, the city looks dull.

More than that, and here we get down to the first problem, if a city's streets are safe from barbarism and fear, the city is thereby tolerably safe from barbarism and fear. When people say that a city, or a part of it, is dangerous or is a jungle what they mean primarily is that they do not feel safe on the sidewalks.

But sidewalks and those who use them are not passive beneficiaries of safety or helpless victims of danger. Sidewalks, their bordering uses, and their users, are active participants in the drama of civilization versus barbarism in cities. To keep the city safe is a fundamental task of a city's streets and its sidewalks.

* * *

The first thing to understand is that the public peace—the sidewalk and street peace—of cities is not kept primarily by the police, necessary as police are. It is kept primarily by an intricate, almost unconscious, network of voluntary controls and standards among the people themselves, and enforced by the people themselves. In some city areas—older public housing projects and streets with very high population turnover are often conspicuous examples—the keeping of public sidewalk law order is left almost entirely to the police and special guards. Such places are jungles. No amount of police can enforce civilization where the normal, casual enforcement of it has broken down.

* * *

This is something everyone already knows: A well-used city street is apt to be a safe street. A deserted city street is apt to be unsafe. But how does this work, really? And what makes a city street well used or shunned? Why is the sidewalk mall in Washington Houses, which is supposed to be an attraction, shunned? Why are the sidewalks of the old city just to its west not shunned? What about streets that are busy part of the time and then empty abruptly?

A city street equipped to handle strangers, and to make a safety asset, in itself, out of the presence of strangers, as the streets of successful city neighborhoods always do, must have three main qualities:

First, there must be a clear demarcation between what is public space and what is private space. Public and private spaces cannot ooze into each other as they do typically in suburban settings or in projects.

Second, there must be eyes upon the street, eyes belonging to those we might call the natural proprietors of the street. The buildings on a street equipped to handle strangers and to insure the safety of both residents and strangers, must be oriented to the street. They cannot turn their backs or blank sides on it and leave it blind.

And third, the sidewalk must have users on it fairly continuously, both to add to the number of effective eyes on the street and to induce the people in buildings along the street to watch the sidewalks in sufficient numbers. Nobody enjoys sitting on a stoop or looking out a window at an empty street. Almost nobody does such a thing. Large numbers of people entertain themselves, off and on, by watching street activity.

Tent City, USA

Maria L. La Ganga

Born in Caldwell, New Jersey, Maria La Ganga currently lives in the San Francisco Bay Area. She has been a staff writer for the Los Angeles Times *since 2007, writing stories on a variety of issues, including a proposed ban on pet sales in San Francisco, early Chinese immigration to the Bay Area, and the rioting that followed the involuntary manslaughter conviction of a white transit officer charged with shooting an unarmed black man at a Bay Area Rapid Transit (BART) station. In the following selection, La Ganga recounts her visits to a Sacramento tent city, where she interviewed residents and reported on efforts by humanitarian agencies and government officials to deal with the situation.*

1 The capital's tent city sprawls messily on a grassed-over landfill beneath power lines, home to some two hundred men and women with nowhere else to go. It has been here for more than a year, but in the last three weeks it has transformed into a vivid symbol of a financial crisis otherwise invisible to most Americans.

The Depression had Hoovervilles. The energy crisis had snaking gas lines. The state's droughts have empty reservoirs and brown lawns. But today's deep recession is largely about disappearing wealth—painful, yes, but difficult to see. Then this tattered encampment along the American River began showing up on *Oprah Winfrey,* All Jazeera, and other news outlets around the world. On Thursday, city officials announced that they will shut it down within a month. "We're finding other places to go," said Steven Maviglio, a spokesman for Sacramento's mayor. The camp is "not safe. It's not humane. But we're not going in with a bulldozer."

Reprinted by permission from *Los Angeles Times,* March 20, 2009.

The ragtag community captured the collective imagination through a powerful combination of geography, celebrity, and journalistic convenience. "This is the state capital of the seventh-largest economy in the world, with a movie-star governor, Arnold Schwarzenegger, and an NBA pro-athlete for a new mayor, Kevin Johnson," said Barbara O'Connor, director of the Institute for the Study of Politics and Media at Cal State Sacramento. And the camp "is a wonderful visual for TV journalists."

On a recent chilly morning in the tent city, it is not yet sunrise. A Fox News van is parked nearby. A flashlight illuminates the inside of a dome tent. Traffic whines along the adjacent freeway. Cats criss-cross the encampment, eyes glowing. As the sky slowly lightens, shadowy figures emerge and head for the bushes along the riverbank. There are no portable toilets. The dumpster is a new arrival, a donation that followed the flood of news reports.

Jim Gibson heads to a neighboring tent, where two of his friends —an unemployed car salesman married to a onetime truck driver— are brewing coffee on a propane stove. Gibson looks like anybody's sunburned suburban dad, all jeans, polar fleece, and sleepy eyes, his neatly trimmed hair covered by a ball cap. Seven months ago, the fifty-year-old contractor had a job and an apartment in Sacramento. Today, he struggles to stay clean and fed. A former owner of the American dream, he is living the American nightmare. In 2004, Gibson was a semi-retired San Jose homeowner, who got bored and wanted to go back to work. Five years, two houses, and four layoffs later, the widower and grandfather says he is "trying to survive and look for work. The only work I've found is holding an advertising sign on a street corner."

Survival is the biggest time-filler here. Tents must be shored up against wind and rain. The schedule for meals, clothing giveaways, and shower times at local agencies must be strictly followed. CeCe Walker, forty-eight, is just back from coffee, breakfast, and a shower at Maryhouse, a daytime shelter for women. She has lugged a bag of ice for half a mile and cleans out a cooler with "Hobo Fridge" written on the side in thick black marker. "I've never camped in my life," she says, sorting through supplies damp from yesterday's melted ice. "This will make you old. I don't see how people want to live out here forever. God!" The tent city sprawls along the river in small clusters of ersatz neighborhoods. Walker and her neighbor, Charly Hine, thirty-eight, have pitched their tents at the distant edge to stay away from noise and trouble. Gibson's tent is in a separate, small, neat grouping. One neighbor displays an American flag and a goose with the word "welcome" on its breast. It is a favorite subject, its owner says, of news photographers. Another has a mailbox and a gate.

The largest and most raucous neighborhood is composed of about seventy tents closest to the street. Near noon, Tammie and Keith Day are drinking beer around a cold fire pit, worrying about how she'll get her diabetes medication and fretting about whether officials will shutter the tent city. "We're homeless and being evicted?" Tammie fumes. "Now I've heard everything." Keith has rheumatoid arthritis. Tammie says they both battle mental illness and alcoholism. Soon, they are in a screaming fight, hurling epithets and bricks at each other. The bricks, at least, miss their marks.

One downside to all the media attention, Tammie says before the brawl, is that her family no longer pays for her prescription. They have seen the news. Her brother is "disgusted." And her mother "doesn't even talk to me now." But an upside rolls up the dusty path about 3:30: a white Toyota pickup from the Florin Worship Center, with volunteers distributing dinner—pasta, potatoes and eggs scrambled together, beans. A maroon Ford Expedition is next, with free tents. A Roseville handyman arrives with firewood.

On this day, Sister Libby Fernandez, executive director of the homeless support group Loaves & Fishes, and attorney Cathleen Williams have convened a meeting of the tent city's leadership council. They sit on a dusty footpath under a tree and talk about the future. Fernandez says she has to return a call back at the office. "Maria Shriver wants to know what the hell is going on," she says. "I'll tell her we need Porta-Potties." Last week, the city announced that it could clear out the tent city in fourteen days but backed off after the mayor called an emergency summit meeting among city officials, homeless advocates, and leaders in the homeless population. But after summit meeting No. 2 on Thursday, he announced various new measures, among them finding more shelter beds for the tent city's residents and studying the feasibility of a permanent encampment. But not where it is now. By April 30, he said, this one must close. "The fact that we have all this attention, people have asked me if I think it's a negative and a stain for the city," Johnson said, in a recent interview. "Now that we have a spotlight shining . . . it allows us to fix it."

10 Fernandez figures that about four-fifths of the tent city's residents have been homeless for more than a year. Many of them are people like Preston Anderson, fifty-seven, who would be happy if he never slept under a roof again. He has his dogs. He feeds stale croissants to wild birds and supports himself by scavenging cans. "Nobody bothers me," he said. "I'm free." The rest—a growing number—are recession victims, such as Boyd Zimmerman and his fiancee, Christina Hopper.

It is 4 P.M. The wind picks up and the shadows lengthen. Zimmerman is trying to help neighbors Jeffrey and Louise Staal pitch a big new tent. They are defeated by the gusts. Zimmerman and Hopper have lived in the tent city for the last seven months. In Phoenix, he had a job driving contract laborers from one work site to another. They owned a double-wide trailer. Then work dried up. They sold their home "for almost nothing" and headed to Sacramento, where Zimmerman grew up. He's one of the lucky ones. He got a paying job at Loaves & Fishes and is saving to rent an apartment. "I have a AAA card," he says ruefully as the sun sinks. "I'm middle-class. . . . I have to get the heck out of here. It's not a good life."

Where Worlds Collide

Pico Iyer

Pico Iyer (1957–) was born in Oxford, England and experienced the education reserved for Britain's elite: at Eton, an exclusive prep school; at Oxford, the most distinguished university in England; and later at Harvard, the most revered university in America. Iyer writes for Time, The Village Voice, *and other magazines. His travel book,* Video Night in Kathmandu, and Other Reports from the Not-so-far-East *(1988), was widely praised. He has written two more travel books,* The Lady and the Monk *(1991) and* Falling off the Map *(1993). He currently lives in Santa Barbara, California.In the following selection from* Harper's, *Iyer describes the cross-cultural chaos of life at the Los Angeles International Airport, where "everyone is a stranger in our new floating world."*

1 They come out, blinking, into the bleached, forgetful sunshine, 1
in Dodgers caps and Rodeo Drive T-shirts, with the maps their cousins have drawn for them and the images they've brought over from *Cops* and *Terminator 2*; they come out, dazed, disoriented, heads still partly in the clouds, bodies still several time zones—or centuries—away, and they step into the Promised Land.

In front of them is a Van Stop, a Bus Stop, a Courtesy Tram Stop, and a Shuttle Bus Stop (the shuttles themselves tracing circuits A, B, and C). At the Shuttle Bus Stop, they see the All American Shuttle, the Apollo Shuttle, Celebrity Airport Livery, the Great American Stageline, the Movie Shuttle, the Transport, Ride-4-You, and forty-two other magic buses waiting to whisk them everywhere from Bakersfield to Disneyland. They see Koreans piling into the Taeguk Airport Shuttle and the Seoul Shuttle, which will take them to Kore-

---

Reprinted from *Harper's Magazine*, August 1995, by permission of Janklow & Nesbit Associates, Inc.

atown without their ever feeling they've left home; they see newcomers from the Middle East disappearing under the Arabic script of the Sahara Shuttle. They see fast-talking, finger-snapping, palm-slapping jive artists straight from their TV screens shouting incomprehensible slogans about deals, destinations, and drugs. Over there is a block-long white limo, a Lincoln Continental, and, over there, a black Chevy Blazer with Mexican stickers all over its windows, being towed. They have arrived in the Land of Opportunity, and the opportunities are swirling dizzily, promiscuously, around them.

They have already braved the ranks of Asian officials, the criminal-looking security men in jackets that say "Elsinore Airport Services," the men shaking tins that say "Helping America's Hopeless." They have already seen the tilting mugs that say "California: a new slant on life" and the portable fruit machines in the gift shop. They have already, perhaps, visited the rest room where someone has written, "Yes on Proposition 187. Mexicans go home," the snack bar where a slice of pizza costs $3.19 (18 quetzals, they think in horror, or 35,000 dong), and the sign that urges them to try the Cockatoo Inn Grand Hotel. The latest arrivals at Los Angeles International Airport are ready now to claim their new lives.

Above them in the terminal, voices are repeating, over and over, in Japanese, Spanish, and unintelligible English, "Maintain visual contact with your personal property at all times." Out on the sidewalk, a man's voice and a woman's voice are alternating an unending refrain: "The white zone is for loading and unloading of passengers only. No parking." There are "Do Not Cross" yellow lines cordoning off parts of the sidewalk and "Wells Fargo Alarm Services" stickers on the windows; there are "Aviation Safeguard" signs on the baggage carts and "Beware of Solicitors" signs on the columns; there are even special phones "To Report Trouble." More male and female voices are intoning, continuously, "Do not leave your car unattended" and "Unattended cars are subject to immediate tow-away." There are no military planes on the tarmac here, the newcomers notice, no khaki soldiers in fatigues, no instructions not to take photographs, as at home; but there are civilian restrictions every bit as strict as in many a police state.

5 "This Terminal Is in a Medfly Quarantine Area," says the sign between the terminals. "Stop the Spread of Medfly!" If, by chance, the new Americans have to enter a parking lot on their way out, they will be faced with "Cars left over 30 days may be impounded at

Owner's Expense" and "Do not enter without a ticket." It will cost them $16 if they lose their parking ticket, they read, and $56 if they park in the wrong zone. Around them is an unending cacophony of antitheft devices, sirens, beepers, and car-door openers; lights are flashing everywhere, and the man who fines them $16 for losing their parking ticket has the tribal scars of Tigre across his forehead.

The blue skies and palm trees they saw on TV are scarcely visible from here: just an undifferentiated smoggy haze, billboards advertising Nissan and Panasonic and Canon, and beyond those an endlessly receding mess of gray streets. Overhead, they can see the all-too-familiar signs of Hilton and Hyatt and Holiday Inn; in the distance, a sea of tract houses, mini-malls, and high-rises. The City of Angels awaits them.

It is a commonplace nowadays to say that cities look more and more like airports, cross-cultural spaces that are a gathering of tribes and races and variegated tongues; and it has always been true that airports are in many ways like miniature cities, whole, self-sufficient communities, with their own chapels and museums and gymnasiums. Not only have airports colored our speech (teaching us about being upgraded, bumped, and put on standby, coaching us in the ways of fly-by-night operations, holding patterns, and the Mile High Club); they have also taught us their own rules, their own codes, their own customs. We eat and sleep and shower in airports; we pray and weep and kiss there. Some people stay for days at a time in these perfectly convenient, hermetically sealed, climate-controlled duty-free zones, which offer a kind of caesura from the obligations of daily life.

Airports are also, of course, the new epicenters and paradigms of our dawning post-national age—not just the bus terminals of the global village but the prototypes, in some sense, for our polyglot, multicolored, user-friendly future. And in their very universality—like the mall, the motel, or the McDonald's outlet—they advance the notion of a future in which all the world's a multiculture. If you believe that more and more of the world is a kind of mongrel hybrid in which many cities (Sydney, Toronto, Singapore) are simply suburbs of a single universal order, then Los Angeles's LAX, London's Heathrow, and Hong Kong's Kai Tak are merely stages on some great global Circle Line, shuttling variations on a common global theme. Mass travel has made L.A. contiguous to Seoul and adjacent to Sao Paulo, and has made all of them now feel a little like bedroom communities for Tokyo.

And as with most social trends, especially th
tomorrow, what is true of the world is doubly true
what is doubly true of America is quadruply true
L.A., legendarily, has more Thais than any city bu
Koreans than any city but Seoul, more El Salvador
outside of San Salvador, more Druze than anywhere but Beirut; it is, at the very least, the easternmost outpost of Asia and the northernmost province of Mexico. When I stopped at a Traveler's Aid desk at LAX recently, I was told I could request help in Khamu, Mien, Tigrinya, Tajiki, Pashto, Dari, Pangasinan, Pampangan, Waray-Waray, Bambara, Twi, and Bicolano (as well, of course, as French, German, and eleven languages from India). LAX is as clear an image as exists today of the world we are about to enter, and of the world that's entering us.

10 For me, though, LAX has always had a more personal resonance: it was in LAX that I arrived myself as a new immigrant, in 1966; and from the time I was in the fourth grade, it was to LAX that I would go three times a year, as an "Unaccompanied minor," to fly to school in London—and to LAX that I returned three times a year for my holidays. Sometimes it seems as if I have spent half my life in LAX. For me, it is the site of my liberation (from school, from the Old World, from home) and the place where I came to design my own new future.

Often when I have set off from L.A. to some distant place—Havana, say, or Hanoi, or Pyongyang—I have felt that the multicultural drama on display in LAX, the interaction of exoticism and familiarity, was just as bizarre as anything I would find when I arrived at my foreign destination. The airport is an Amy Tan novel, a short story by Bharati Mukherjee, a Henry James sketch set to an MTV beat; it is a cross-generational saga about Chang Hsieng meeting his daughter Cindy and finding that she's wearing a nose ring now and is shacked up with a surfer from Berlin. The very best kind of airport reading to be found in LAX these days is the triple-decker melodrama being played out all around one—a complex tragicomedy of love and war and exile, about people fleeing centuries-old rivalries and thirteenth-century mullahs and stepping out into a fresh, forgetful, born-again city that is rewriting its script every moment.

Not long ago I went to spend a week in LAX. I haunted the airport by day and by night, I joined the gloomy drinkers listening to air-control-tower instructions on ear-phones at the Proud Bird bar. I listened each morning to Airport Radio (530 AM), and I slept each night at the Airport Sheration or the Airport Hilton. I lived off cellophaned crackers and Styrofoam cups of tea, browsed for hours among Best Actor statuettes and Beverly Hills magnets, and tried to see what kinds of America the city presents to the new Americans, who are remaking America each day.

It is almost too easy to say that LAX is a perfect metaphor for L.A., a flat, spaced-out desert kind of place, highly automotive, not deeply hospitable, with little reading matter and no organizing principle. (There are eight satellites without a center here, many international arrivals are shunted out into the bleak basement of Terminal 2, and there is no airline that serves to dominate LAX as Pan Am once did JFK.) Whereas "SIN" is a famously ironical airline code for Singapore, cathedral of puritanical rectitude, "LAX" has always seemed perilously well chosen for a city whose main industries were traditionally thought to be laxity and relaxation. LAX is at once a vacuum waiting to be colonized and a joyless theme park—Tomorrowland, Adventureland, and Fantasyland all at once.

The postcards on sale here (made in Korea) dutifully call the airport "one of the busiest and most beautiful air facilities in the world," and it is certainly true that LAX, with thirty thousand international arrivals each day—roughly the same number of tourists that have visited the Himalayan country of Bhutan in its entire history—is not uncrowded. But bigger is less and less related to better: in a recent survey of travel facilities, *Business Traveller* placed LAX among the five worst airports in the world for customs, luggage retrieval, and passport processing.

15 LAX is, in fact, a surprisingly shabby and hollowed-out kind of place, certainly not adorned with the amenities one might expect of the world's strongest and richest power. When you come out into the Arrivals area in the International Terminal, you will find exactly one tiny snack bar, which serves nine items; of them, five are identified as Cheese Dog, Chili Dog, Chili Cheese Dog, Nachos with Cheese, and Chili Cheese Nachos. There is a large panel on the wall offering rental-car services and hotels, and the newly deplaned American dreamer can choose between the Cadillac Hotel, the Banana Bungalow (which offers a Basketball Court, "Free Toast," "Free Bed Sheets," and "Free Movies and Parties"), and the Backpacker's Paradise (with "Free Afternoon Tea and Crumpets" and "Free Evening Party Including Food and Champagne").

Around one in the terminal is a swirl of priests rattling cans, Iranians in suits brandishing pictures of torture victims, and Japanese girls in Goofy hats. "I'm looking for something called Clearasil," a distinguished-looking Indian man diffidently tells a cashier. "Clearasil?" shouts the girl. "For your face?"

Upstairs, in the Terrace Restaurant, passengers are gulping down "Dutch Chocolate" and "Japanese Coffee" while students translate back and forth between English and American, explaining that "soliciting" loses something of its cachet when you go across the Atlantic. A fat man is nuzzling the neck of his outrageously pretty Filipina companion, and a few Brits are staring doubtfully at the sign that assures them that seafood is "cheerfully served at your table!" Only in America, they are doubtless thinking. A man goes from table to table, plunking down on each one a key chain attached to a globe. As soon as an unsuspecting customer picks one up, touched by the largesse of the New World and convinced now that there is such a thing as a free lunch in America, the man appears again, flashes a sign that says "I Am a Deaf," and requests a dollar for the gift.

At a bank of phones, a saffron-robed monk gingerly inserts a credit card, while schoolkids page Jesse Jackson at the nearest "white courtesy telephone." One notable feature of the modern airport is that it is wired, with a vengeance: even in a tiny, two-urinal men's room, I found two telephones on offer; LAX bars rent out cellular phones; and in the Arrivals area, as you come out into the land of plenty, you face a bank of forty-six phones of every kind, with screens and buttons and translations, from which newcomers are calling direct to Bangalore or Baghdad. Airports are places for connections of all kinds and *loci classici*, perhaps, for a world ruled by IDD and MCI, DOS and JAL.

Yet for all these grounding reminders of the world outside, everywhere I went in the airport I felt myself in an odd kind of twilight zone of consciousness, that weightless limbo of a world in which people are between lives and between selves, almost sleepwalking, not really sure of who or where they are. Light-headed from the trips they've taken, ears popping and eyes about to do so, under a potent foreign influence, people are at the far edge of themselves in airports, ready to break down or through. You see strangers pouring out their life stories to strangers here, or making new life stories with other strangers. Everything is at once intensified and slightly unreal. One L.A. psychiatrist advises shy women to practice their flirting here, and religious groups circle in the hope of catching unattached souls.

20 Airports, which often have a kind of perpetual morning-after feeling (the end of the holiday, the end of the affair), are places where everyone is ruled by the clock, but all the clocks show different times. These days, after all, we fly not only into yesterday or this morning when we go across the world but into different decades, often, of the world's life and our own: in ten or fifteen hours, we are taken back into the twelfth century or into worlds we haven't seen since childhood. And in the process we are subjected to transitions more jolting than any imagined by Oscar Wilde or Sigmund Freud: if the average individual today sees as many images in a day as a Victorian saw in a lifetime, the average person today also has to negotiate switches between continents inconceivable only fifty years ago. Frequent fliers like Ted Turner have actually become ill from touching down and taking off so often; but, in less diagnosable ways, all of us are being asked to handle difficult suspensions of the laws of Nature and Society when moving between competing worlds.

This helps to compound the strange statelessness of airports, where all bets are off and all laws are annulled—modern equivalents, perhaps, to the hundred yards of no-man's-land between two frontier crossings. In airports we are often in dreamy, floating, out-of-body states, as ready to be claimed as that suitcase on Carousel C. Even I, not traveling, didn't know sometimes if I was awake or asleep in LAX, as I heard an announcer intone, "John Cheever, John Cheever, please contact a Northwest representative in the Baggage Claim area. John Cheever, please contact a service representative at the Northwest Baggage Claim area."

As I started to sink into this odd, amphibious, bipolar state, I could begin to see why a place like LAX is a particular zone of fear, more terrifying to many people than anywhere but the dentist's office. Though dying in a plane is, notoriously, twenty times less likely than dying in a car, every single airline crash is front-page news and so dramatic—not a single death but three hundred—that airports are for many people killing grounds. Their runways are associated in the mind's (televisual) eye with hostages and hijackings; with bodies on the tarmac or antiterrorist squads storming the plane.

That general sense of unsettledness is doubtless intensified by all the people in uniform in LAX. There are ten different security agencies working the Tom Bradley Terminal alone, and the streets outside are jam-packed with Airport Police cars, FBI men, and black-clad airport policemen on bicycles. All of them do as much, I suspect, to instill fear as to still it. "People are scared here," a gloomy Pakistani security guard told me, "because undercover are working. Police are working. You could be undercover, I could be undercover. Who knows?"

And just as L.A. is a province of the future in part because so many people take it to be the future, so it is a danger zone precisely because it is imagined to be dangerous. In Osaka's new $16 billion airport recently, I cross-examined the Skynet computer (in the Departures area) about what to expect when arriving at LAX or any other foreign airport. "Guard against theft in the arrival hall," it told me (and, presumably, even warier Japanese). "A thief is waiting for a chance to take advantage of you." Elsewhere it added, "Do not dress too touristy," and, "Be on your guard when approached by a group of suspicious-looking children, such as girls wearing bright-colored shirts and scarves." True to such dark prognostications, the side doors of the Airport Sheraton at LAX are locked every day from 8:00 P.M. to 6:00 A.M., and you cannot even activate the elevators without a room key. "Be extra careful in parking garages and stairwells," the hotel advises visitors. "Always try to use the main entrance to your hotel, particularly late in the evening. Never answer your hotel room door without verifying who is there."

25 One reason airports enjoy such central status in our imaginations is that they play such a large part in forming our first (which is sometimes our last) impression of a place; this is the reason that poor countries often throw all their resources into making their airports sleek, with beautifully landscaped roads leading out of them into town. L.A., by contrast, has the bareness of arrogance, or simple inhospitability. Usually what you see as you approach the city is a grim penitential haze through which is visible nothing but rows of gray buildings, a few dun-hued warehouses, and ribbons of dirty freeway: a no-colored blur without even the comforting lapis omaments of the swimming pools that dot New York or Johannesburg. (Ideally, in fact, one should enter L.A. by night, when the whole city pulses like an electric grid of lights—or the back of a transistor radio, in Thomas Pynchon's inspired metaphor. While I was staying in LAX, Jackie Collins actually told Los Angeles magazine that "Flying in [to LAX] at night is just an orgasmic thrill.") You land, with a bump, on a mess of gray runways with no signs of welcome, a hangar that says "TransWorld Airlines," another broken sign that announces "Tom Bradly International Airport," and an air-control tower under scaffolding.

The first thing that greeted me on a recent arrival was a row of Asians sitting on the floor of the terminal, under a sign that told them of a $25,000 fine for bringing in the wrong kinds of food. As I passed through endless corridors, I was faced with almost nothing except long escalators (a surprisingly high percentage of the accidents recorded at airports comes from escalators, bewildering to newcomers) and bare hallways. The other surprise, for many of my fellow travelers, no doubt, was that almost no one we saw looked like Robert Redford or Julia Roberts or, indeed, like anyone belonging to the race we'd been celebrating in our in-flight movies. As we passed into the huge, bare assembly hall that is the Customs and Immigration Center here, I was directed into one of the chaotic lines by a Noriko and formally admitted to the country by a C. Chen. The man waiting to transfer my baggage (as a beagle sniffed around us in a coat that said "Agricultre's Beagle Brigade" on one side and "Protecting American Agriculture" on the other) was named Yoji Yosaka. And the first sign I saw, when I stepped into America, was a big board being waved by the "Executive Sedan Service" for one "Mr. T. Ego."

For many immigrants, in fact, LAX is quietly offering them a view of their own near futures: the woman at the Host Coffee Shop is themselves, in a sense, two years from now, and the man sweeping up the refuse is the American dream in practice. The staff at the airport seems to be made up almost entirely of recent immigrants: on my very first afternoon there, I was served by a Hoa, an Ephraim, and a Glinda; the wait-people at a coffee shop in Terminal 5 were called Ignacio, Ever, Aura, and Erick. Even at the Airport Sheraton (where the employees all wear nameplates), I was checked in by Viera (from "Bratislavia") and ran into Hasmik and Yovik (from Ethiopia), Faye (from Vietnam), Ingrid (from Guatemala City), Khrystyne (from Long Beach, by way of Phnom Penh, I think), and Moe (from West L.A., she said). Many of the bright-eyed dreamers who arrive at LAX so full of hope never actually leave the place.

The deeper drama of any airport is that it features a kind of interaction almost unique in our lives, wherein many of us do not know whom we are going to meet or whom others are going to meet in us. You see people standing at the barriers outside the Customs area looking into their pasts, while wide-open newcomers drift out, searching for their futures. Lovers do not know if they will see the same person who kissed them good-bye a month ago; grandparents wonder what the baby they last saw twenty years ago will look like now.

In L.A. all of this has an added charge, because unlike many cities, it is not a hub but a terminus: a place where people come to arrive. Thus many of the meetings you witness are between the haves and the hope-to-haves, between those who are affecting a new ease in their new home and those who are here in search of that ease. Both parties, especially if they are un-American by birth, are eager to stress their Americanness or their fitness for America; and both, as they look at each other's made-up self, see themselves either before or after a stay in L.A.'s theater of transformation. And so they stream in, wearing running shoes or cowboy hats or 49ers jackets, anxious to make a good first impression; and the people who wait for them, under a halfhearted mural of Desertland, are often American enough not to try to look the part. Juan and Esperanza both have ponytails now, and Kimmie is wearing a Harley-Davidson cap backwards and necking with a Japanese guy; the uncle from Delhi arrives to find that Rajiv not only has grown darker but has lost weight, so that he looks more like a peasant from back home than ever.

30 And the newcomers pour in in astonishing numbers. A typical 30
Sunday evening, in a single hour, sees flights arriving from England, Taiwan, the Philippines, Indonesia, Mexico, Austria, Germany, Spain, Costa Rica, and Guatemala; and each new group colors and transforms the airport: an explosion of tropical shades from Hawaiian Air, a rash of blue blazers and white shirts around the early flight from Tokyo. Red-haired Thais bearing pirated Schwarzenegger videos, lonely Africans in Aerial Assault sneakers, farmers from changeless Confucian cultures peering into the smiles of a Prozac city, children whose parents can't pronounce their names. Many of them are returning, like Odysseus, with the spoils of war: young brides from Luzon, business cards from Shanghai, boxes of macadamia nuts from Oahu. And for many of them the whole wild carnival will feature sights they have never seen before: Japanese look anxiously at the first EI Salvadorans they've ever seen, and EI Salvadorans ogle sleek girls from Bangkok in thigh-high boots. All of them, moreover, may not be pleased to realize that the America they've dreamed of is, in fact, a land of tacos and pita and pad thai—full, indeed, of the very Third World cultures that other Third Worlders look down upon.

One day over lunch I asked my Ethiopian waitress about her life here. She liked it well enough, she said, but still she missed her home. And yet, she added, she couldn't go back. "Why not?" I asked, still smiling. "Because they killed my family," she said. "Two years back.

They killed my father. They killed my brother." "They," I realized, referred to the Tigreans—many of them working just down the corridor in other parts of the hotel. So, too, Tibetans who have finally managed to flee their Chinese-occupied homeland arrive at LAX to find Chinese faces everywhere; those who fled the Sandinistas find themselves standing next to Sandinistas fleeing their successors. And all these people from ancient cultures find themselves in a country as amnesiac as the morning, where World War II is just a rumor and the Gulf War a distant memory. Their pasts are escaped, yes, but by the same token they are unlikely to be honored.

It is dangerously tempting to start formulating socioeconomic principles in the midst of LAX: people from rich countries (Germany and Japan, say) travel light, if only because they are sure that they can return any time; those from poor countries come with their whole lives in cardboard boxes imperfectly tied with string. People from poor countries are often met by huge crowds—for them each arrival is a special occasion—and stagger through customs with string bags and Gold Digger apple crates, their addresses handwritten on them in pencil; the Okinawan honeymooners, by contrast, in the color coordinated outfits they will change every day, somehow have packed all their needs into a tiny case.

If airports have some of the excitement of bars, because so many people are composing (and decomposing) selves there, they also have some of the sadness of bars, the poignancy of people sitting unclaimed while everyone around them has paired off. A pretty girl dressed in next to nothing sits alone in an empty Baggage Claim area, waiting for a date who never comes; a Vietnamese man, lost, tells an official that he has friends in Orange County who can help him, but when the friends are contacted, they say they know no one from Vietnam. I hear of a woman who got off and asked for "San Mateo," only to learn that she was meant to disembark in San Francisco; and a woman from Nigeria who came out expecting to see her husband in Monroe, Louisiana, only to learn that someone in Lagos had mistaken "La." on her itinerary for "L.A."

The greetings I saw in the Arrivals area were much more tentative than I had expected, less passionate—as ritualized in their way as the kisses placed on Bob Barker's cheek—and much of that may be because so many people are meeting strangers, even if they are meeting people they once knew. Places like LAX—places like L.A.—perpetuate the sense that everyone is a stranger in our new floating world. I spent one afternoon in the airport with a Californian blonde, and I saw her complimented on her English by a sweet Korean woman and asked by an Iranian if she was Indian. Airports have some of the unsteady brashness of singles bars, where no one knows quite what is expected of them. "Mike, is that you?" "Oh, I didn't recognize you." "I'd have known you anywhere." "It's so kind of you to come and pick me up." And already at a loss, a young Japanese girl and a broad, lonely-looking man head off toward the parking lot, not knowing, in any sense, who is going to be in the driver's seat.

35 The driving takes place, of course, in what many of the newcomers, primed by video screenings of L.A. Law and Speed, regard as the ultimate heart of darkness, a place at least as forbidding and dangerous as Africa must have seemed to the Victorians. They have heard about how America is the murder capital of the world; they have seen Rodney King get pummeled by L.A.'s finest; they know of the city as the site of drive-by shootings and freeway snipers, of riots and celebrity murders. The "homeless" and the "tempest-tost" that the Statue of Liberty invites are arriving, increasingly, in a city that is itself famous for its homeless population and its fires, floods, and earthquakes.

In that context, the ideal symbol of LAX is, perhaps, the great object that for thirty years has been the distinctive image of the place: the ugly white quadruped that sits in the middle of the airport like a beached white whale or a jet-age beetle, featuring a 360-degree circular restaurant that does not revolve and an observation deck from which the main view is of twenty-three thousand parking places. The Theme Building, at 201 World Way, is a sad image of a future that never arrived, a monument to Kennedy-era idealism and the thrusting modernity of the American empire when it was in its prime; it now has the poignancy of an abandoned present with its price tag stuck to it. When you go there (and almost nobody does) you are greeted by photos of Saturn's rings and Jupiter and its moons, by a plaque laid down by L.B.J. and a whole set of symbols from the time when NASA was shooting for the heavens. Now the "landmark" building, with its "gourmet-type restaurant," looks like a relic from a time long past, when it must have looked like the face of the future.

Upstairs, a few desperately merry waiters are serving nonalcoholic drinks and cheeseburgers to sallow diners who look as if they've arrived at the end of the world; on the tarmac outside, speedbirds inch ahead like cars in a traffic jam. "Hello All the New People of LAX—Welcome," says the graffiti on the elevator.

The Theme Restaurant comes to us from an era when L.A. was leading the world. Nowadays, of course, L.A. is being formed and reformed and led by the world around it. And as I got ready to leave LAX, I could not help but feel that the Theme Building stands, more and more, for a city left behind by our accelerating planet. LAX, I was coming to realize, was a good deal scruffier than the airports even of Bangkok or Jakarta, more chaotic, more suggestive of Third World lawlessness. And the city around it is no more golden than Seoul, no more sunny than Taipei, and no more laid-back than Moscow. Beverly Hills, after all, is largely speaking Farsi now. Hollywood Boulevard is sleazier than 42nd Street. And Malibu is falling into the sea.

Yet just as I was about to give up on L.A. as yesterday's piece of modernity, I got on the shuttle bus that moves between the terminals in a never-ending loop. The seats next to me were taken by two tough-looking dudes from nearby South Central, who were riding the free buses and helping people on and off with their cases (acting, I presumed, on the safe assumption that the Japanese, say, new to the country and bewildered, had been warned beforehand to tip often and handsomely for every service they received). In between terminals, as a terrified-looking Miss Kudo and her friend guarded their luggage, en route from Nagoya to Las Vegas, the two gold-plated sharks talked about the Raiders' last game and the Lakers' next season. Then one of them, without warning, announced, "The bottom line is the spirit is with you. When you work out, you chill out and, like, you meditate in your spirit. You know what I mean? Meditation is recreation. Learn math, follow your path. That's all I do, man, that's all I live for: learnin' about God, learnin' about Jesus. I am possessed by that spirit. You know, I used to have all these problems, with the flute and all, but when I heard about God, I learned about the body, the mind, and the flesh. People forget, they don't know, that the Bible isn't talkin' about the flesh, it's talkin' about the spirit. And I was reborn again in the spirit."

His friend nodded. "When you recreate, you meditate. Recreation is a spiritually uplifting experience."

"Yeah. When you do that, you allow the spirit to breathe."

"Because you're gettin' into the physical world. You're lettin' the spirit flow. You're helpin' the secretion of the endorphins in the brain."

Nearby, the Soldiers of the Cross of Christ Church stood by the escalators, taking donations, and a man in a dog collar approached another stranger.

I watched the hustlers allowing the spirit to breathe, I heard the Hare Krishna devotees plying their wares, I spotted some Farrakhan flunkies collecting a dollar for a copy of their newspaper, The Final Call—redemption and corruption all around us in the air—and I thought: welcome to America, Miss Kudo, welcome to L.A.

Unit 2

Unit 2 Defining Lines

Issues of national boundaries and immigration are on the front pages of our newspapers every day. In this context, borders serve to include and exclude, define and redefine. In this unit, we will explore the concept of our national borders and the controversies surrounding issues of immigration and acculturation.

★ ★ ★

Immigration Myths and Facts

American Civil Liberties Union

According to the National Research Council of the National Academy of Sciences, individual immigrants contribute $80,000 more in taxes than they consume in government benefits over the course of their lives. Immigrants not only boost the national economy as a whole, but they also tend to raise the earnings levels of non-immigrants. Latino immigrants learn English at rates comparable to previous waves of immigrants. Even though the process is long and hard, many immigrants seek U.S. citizenship. Even undocumented immigrants pay the same real estate and sales taxes as everyone else, without receiving the government benefits that normally go with them. These facts and more fill this ACLU report on immigrants in American society.

MYTH: Immigrants are a drain on our social services.

FACT: By paying taxes and Social Security, immigrants contribute far more to government coffers than they use in social services.

In its landmark report published in 1997—arguably the most thorough national study to date of immigration's fiscal impacts—the National Research Council (NRC) of the National Academy of Sciences concluded that on average, immigrants generate public revenue that exceeds their public costs over time—approximately $80,000 more in taxes than they receive in state, federal and local benefits over their life times.[1] This same conclusion was reached in 2007 by the Council of Economic Advisers in their report to the Executive Office of the President where they state that "the long-run impact

★ ★ ★ ★ ★ ★

Reprinted from *American Civil Liberties Union*, January 2008.

of immigration on public budgets is likely to be positive," and agree with the NRC report's view that "only a forward-looking projection of taxes and government spending can offer an accurate picture of the long-run fiscal consequences of admitting new immigrants."[2]

Indeed, most non-citizens are not even eligible for the majority of welfare programs unless they are legal permanent residents and have resided in the United States legally for at least five years. This includes benefits such as Temporary Assistance for Needy Families (TANF), SSI, Medicaid, and the State Children's Health Insurance Program (SCHIP).

Moreover, according to government reports, noncitizens are much less likely than citizens to use the benefits for which they are eligible. For example, immigrants, especially the undocumented, tend to use medical services much less than the average American.[3] In fact, the average immigrant uses less than half the dollar amount of health care services as the average native-born citizen.[4] Moreover, the claim that immigrants account for high rates of emergency room (ER) visits is refuted by research; in fact, communities with high rates of ER usage tend to have relatively small percentages of immigrant residents.

Likewise, according to Department of Agriculture reports, noncitizens who are eligible for food stamps are significantly less likely to use them than are all other individuals who are eligible for the program. For example, about 45 percent of eligible noncitizens received food stamps in 2002, compared to almost 60 percent of eligible individuals overall.[5]

Most of the fiscal impact from immigration is felt at the state and local levels. The Council of Economic Advisors points out in its report to the Executive Office of the President that "the positive fiscal impact tends to accrue at the federal level, but the net costs tend to be concentrated at the state and local level," which bear primary responsibility for providing not only health care but education.[6]

Still, according to recent studies from a number of cities and states—including the states of Arizona, Texas, Minnesota, California, New York, North Carolina and Arkansas, and cities or counties of Chicago and Santa Clara—while the cost of educating the children of immigrants may be high, the overall economic benefits of immigrants to the states remain positive.[7] A University of Illinois study found that undocumented immigrants in the Chicago metropolitan area alone spent $2.89 billion in 2001, stimulating an additional $5.45 billion in total local spending and sustaining 31,908 jobs in the local economy.[8]

The Udall Center at the University of Arizona found that the fiscal costs of immigrants, starting with education, totaled $1.41 billion in 2004, which, balanced against $1.64 billion in state tax revenue attributable to immigrants as workers, resulted in a fiscal gain of $222.6 million.[9] Similarly, in its Special

Report about undocumented immigrants in Texas, the Comptroller of Public Accounts found that in 2005, even counting the costs associated with education, "the state revenues collected from undocumented immigrants exceed what the state spent on services, with the difference being $424.7 million."[10]

MYTH: Immigrants have a negative impact on the economy and the wages of citizens and take jobs away from citizens.

FACT: Immigration has a positive effect on the American economy as a whole and on the income of native-born workers.

In June 2007, the President's Council of Economic Advisers (CEA) issued a report on "Immigration's Economic Impact." Based on a thorough review of the literature, the Council concluded that "immigrants not only help fuel the Nation's economic growth, but also have an overall positive effect on the American economy as a whole and on the income of native-born American workers."[11] Among the report's key findings were that, on average, U.S. natives benefit from immigration in that immigrants tend to complement natives, not substitute for them.

Immigrants have different skills, which allow higher-skilled native workers to increase productivity and thus increase their incomes. Also, as the native-born U.S. population becomes older and better educated, young immigrant workers fill gaps in the low-skilled labor markets.[12]

With respect to wages, in a 1997 study, the National Research Council estimated the annual wage gain due to immigration for U.S. workers to be $10 billion each year[13] in 2007 CEA estimated the gain at over $30 billion per year.[14] The CEA acknowledges that an increase in immigrant workers is likely to have some negative impact on the wages of low-skilled native workers, but they found this impact to be relatively small and went on to conclude that reducing immigration "would be a poorly-targeted and inefficient way to assist low-wage Americans."[15]

In addition to having an overall positive affect on the average wages of American workers, an increase in immigrant workers also tends to increase employment rates among the native-born. According to a Pew Hispanic Center study, between 2000 and 2004 "there was a positive correlation between the increase in the foreign-born population and the employment of native-born workers in 27 states and the District of Columbia." These states included all the major destination states for immigrants and together they accounted for 67% of all native-born workers.[16]

California, for example, saw an increase in wages of natives by about four percent from 1990 to 2004—a period of large influx of immigrants to the state—due to the complimentary skills of immigrant workers and an increase in the demand for tasks performed by native workers.[17]

MYTH: Immigrants—particularly Latino immigrants—don't want to learn English.

FACT: Immigrants, including Latino immigrants, believe they need to learn English in order to succeed in the United States, and the majority uses at least some English at work.

Throughout our country's history, critics of immigration have accused new immigrants of refusing to learn English and to otherwise assimilate. These charges are no truer today than they were then. As with prior waves of immigrants, there is a marked increase in English-language skills from one immigrant generation to the next.[18] In the first ever major longitudinal study of the children of immigrants, in 1992 Rambaut and Portes found that "the pattern of linguistic assimilation prevails across nationalities." The authors go on to report that "the linguistic outcomes for the third generation—the grandchildren of the present wave of immigrants—will be little different than what has been the age-old pattern in American immigration history."[19]

While many first-generation Latino immigrants are unable to speak English, 88 percent of their U.S.-born adult children report that they speak English very well.[20] And studies show that the number rises dramatically for each subsequent generation. Furthermore, similar to other immigrants, Latinos believe that they need to learn English in order to succeed in the United States, and believe they will be discriminated against if they don't.[21] Most Latino immigrants (67%) report that they use at least some English at work.[22]

California's second-generation immigrants experience a large drop in "low levels of English proficiency" compared to first generation immigrants, from 27% to 6%, and the proportion of immigrants with high levels of English proficiency rises from 49% in the first generation to 79% in the second generation. The proportion of both Asian and Latino immigrants, who speak English exclusively rises from 10% in the first generation to 29% in the second and 94% in the third.[23] Notwithstanding the current levels of English language acquisition for the newest wave of immigrants, there is a demand for English language classes that far exceeds the supply and which, if met, would greatly advance immigrants' integration into American social and cultural life.

MYTH: Immigrants don't want to become citizens.

FACT: Many immigrants to the United States seek citizenship, even in the face of difficult requirements and huge backlogs that can delay the process for years.

Most immigrants are ineligible to apply for citizenship until they have resided in the U.S. with lawful permanent resident status for five years, have passed background checks, have shown that they have paid their taxes, are of "good moral character, demonstrate knowledge of U.S. history and civics, and have the ability to understand, speak and write English." In addition, people applying for naturalization have to pay a fee, which increased by 69% in 2007 from $400 to $675, making it much harder for low-income immigrants to reach their dream of becoming Americans.[24]

Despite these barriers, The Pew Hispanic Center's report on U.S. Census data shows that the proportion of eligible immigrants who have acquired citizenship rose to 52% in 2005, "the highest level in a quarter of a century."[25] In the 2007 fiscal year, DHS received 1.4 million citizenship applications—nearly double from last fiscal year[26]—and between June and July of 2007, naturalization applications increased 350% compared to last year.[27] In his testimony to Congress, US Citizenship and Immigration Services (USCIS) Director, Emilio Gonzalez, referred to this increase as "unprecedented in the history of immigration services in our nation."[28]

Yet, despite the promise by USCIS that backlogs would be eliminated, applications for naturalization can take a year and half to adjudicate and of the 1.4 applications it received in 2007, less than 660,000 have been decided.[29]

MYTH: Immigrants don't pay taxes.

FACT: Almost all immigrants pay income taxes even though they can't benefit from most federal and state local assistance programs and all immigrants pay sales and property taxes.

According to the 2005 Economic Report of the President, "more than half of all undocumented immigrants are believed to be working 'on the books' . . . [and] . . . contribute to the tax rolls but are ineligible for almost all Federal public assistance programs and most major Federal-state programs." According to the report, undocumented immigrants also "contribute money to public coffers by paying sales and property taxes (the latter are implicit in apartment rentals)."[30]

All immigrants (legal and undocumented) pay the same real estate taxes and the same sales and other consumption taxes as everyone else. The University of Illinois at Chicago found in 2002 that undocumented immigrants in the Chicago metro area spent $2.89 billion annually from their earnings and these expenditures generated $2.56 billion additional spending for the local economy.[31]

Legal immigrants pay income taxes and indeed many undocumented immigrants also pay income taxes or have taxes automatically withheld from their paychecks—even though they are unable to claim a tax refund, Social

Security benefits or other welfare benefits that these taxes support. In the Chicago metro area for example, approximately seventy percent of undocumented workers paid payroll taxes, according to the University of Illinois study from 2002.[32] In the Washington Metro Region, immigrants paid the same share of the region's overall taxes (18 percent) as the rest of the population (17.4 percent), according to a 2006 Urban Institute study.[33] This study also points to the fact that immigrants' tax payments support both local and state services in addition to the federal government.

The Social Security Administration (SSA) holds that undocumented immigrants "account for a major portion" of the billions of dollars paid into the Social Security system—an estimated $520 billion as of October 2005.[34] The SSA keeps a file called the "earnings suspense file" on all earnings with incorrect or fictitious Social Security numbers and the SSA's chief actuary stated in 2005 that "three quarters of other-than-legal immigrants pay payroll taxes."[35] Their figures show that the suspense file is growing by more than $50 billion a year, generating $6 to 7 billion in Social Security tax revenue and about $1.5 billion in Medicare taxes.

MYTH: Immigrants send all their money back to their home countries instead of spending money here.

FACT: Immigrants do send money to family members, making it possible for more people to stay in their home countries rather than migrating to the United States. Importantly, sending remittances home does not keep immigrants from spending money in the United States.

It's true that remittances are the biggest sources of foreign currency for most Latin American countries and surpass any amount of foreign aid sent by the U.S. The money sent by immigrants to their family members allows many people to stay in their home countries who might otherwise feel compelled to migrate to the U.S.

And while 51 percent of Latino immigrants send remittances home,[36] they are spending their money in the United States as well. In fact, a 1998 study found that immigrants become net economic contributors after 10 to 15 years in the U.S.[37]

In addition to paying taxes and Social Security, immigrants spend money on goods and services in the United States. A study of Latino immigrants in California found significant gains in home ownership between those who had been in this country for ten years (16.4 percent are homeowners) and those who had been here for over thirty years (64.6 percent).[38] Furthermore, a 2002 Harvard University study of U.S. Census data found that there were more than 5.7 million foreign-born homeowners in the United States.[39] The study found that foreign-born new homeowners are buying their homes by saving more than native-born homebuyers and stretching their incomes more.

While homeownership nationally was approximately 69% in 2006, it was 60% for Asians and 50% for Latinos—each group with large immigrant populations and therefore greater impediments to obtaining bank loans.[40] Although homeownership is largely correlated with legal status in the U.S., undocumented immigrants are also buying into the "American Dream" of homeownership in some of the most expensive housing markets in the country.[41]

MYTH: Immigrants bring crime to our cities and towns.

FACT: Immigrants are actually far less likely to commit crimes than their native-born counterparts. Even as the undocumented population has increased in the United States, crime rates have decreased significantly.

According to a 2000 report prepared for the U.S. Department of Justice, immigrants maintain low crime rates even when faced with adverse social conditions such as low income and low levels of education.[42]

Although incarceration rates are highest among young low-income men and many immigrants arriving in the U.S. are young men with low levels of education, incarceration rates among young men are invariably lower for immigrants than for their native-born counterparts. This is true across every ethnic group but the differences are especially noticeable among Mexicans, Salvadorans and Guatemalans, who constitute the majority of undocumented immigrants in the United States. Even in cities with the largest immigrant populations, such as New York, Los Angeles, Chicago and Miami, violent and non-violent crime rates have continued to decline.[43]

Even after taking into account higher deportation rates since the mid 1990's, and reviewing the 1980 and 1990 censuses, the National Bureau of Economic Research (NBER) ascertained that, "18-40 year-old male immigrants have lower institutionalization rates than the native born each year . . . and by 2000, immigrants have institutionalization rates that are one-fifth those of the native born."[44] In fact, according to the NBAR study, the newly arrived immigrants are particularly unlikely to be involved in crime.

Cities like Hazleton, Pennsylvania have tried to blame a new wave of immigrants for a supposed rise in crime. Yet, Hazleton's own crime statistics taken from the Pennsylvania State Police show that overall crime in the city has decreased and is now less than half of the national average.[45]

MYTH: Most immigrants are undocumented and have crossed the border illegally.

FACT: Two thirds of immigrants are here lawfully—either as naturalized citizens or in some other lawful status. Moreover, almost half of all undocumented immigrants entered the United States legally.

According to the Pew Hispanic Center, one third of all immigrants are undocumented, one third have some form of legal status and one third are naturalized citizens. This applies to immigrants from Latin America as well as others.[46]

Almost half of all undocumented immigrants entered the United States on visas that allowed them to reside here temporarily—either as tourists, students, or temporary workers. This means they were subject to inspection by immigration officials before entering the country,[47] and became undocumented only when their visas expired and they didn't leave the country.

MYTH: Weak border enforcement has led to high rates of undocumented immigration. We should increase enforcement and build a wall around our border.

FACT: Increased border security and the construction of border fences have done little to curb the flow of immigrants across the United States border. Instead, these policies have only succeeded in pushing border crossers into dangerous and less-patrolled regions, and increased the undocumented population by creating an incentive for immigrants not to leave.

Building a wall along the entire 2000-mile southern U.S. border would be prohibitively expensive. According to a study by the Cato Institute, rather than acting as a deterrent to those attempting to cross the border, increased enforcement has only succeeded in pushing immigration flows into more remote, less patrolled regions, resulting in a tripling of the death rate at the border and decreased apprehensions, and creating a dramatic increase in taxpayer money spent on making arrests along the border (from $300 per arrest in 1992 to $1,200 per arrest in 2002).[48]

Furthermore, increased border enforcement has actually increased the number of undocumented immigrants in the U.S. at any one time. The increased risk and cost to immigrants of crossing the border has resulted in fewer undocumented immigrants returning to their home countries for periods of time as part of the decades-long circular migration patterns that characterize undocumented immigration from Mexico up until the 1990s. Instead, immigrants stay in the United States for longer periods of time, often choosing to immigrate their families to avoid longer periods of separation.[49]

The Secure Fence Act of 2006 directed the Department of Homeland Security to construct 850 miles of additional border fencing. According to a report by Congressional Research Services, the San Diego fence, combined with increased border patrol agents in the area, succeeded in decreasing border crossing in that region, but at the same time there is considerable evidence that the flow of illegal immigration has shifted to the more remote areas of the Arizona desert, decreasing the number of apprehensions and increasing the cost.[50]

Endnotes

[1]National Research Council, The New Americans:Economic, Demographic, and Fiscal Effects of Immigration, ed. James P. Smith and Barry Edmonston (Washington, D.C.:National Academy Press, 1997).

[2]Council of Economic Advisers, "Immigration's Economic Impact," Washington, D.C. June 20, 2007.

[3]Rand Corporation. "Rand Study Shows Relatively Little Public Money Spent Providing Health Care to Undocumented Immigrants," November 2006. http://www.rand.org/news/press.06/11.14.html

[4]Center for Studying Health System Change. "What Accounts for Differences in the Use of Hospital Emergency Departments Across U.S. Communities?" Prepared by Peter Cunningham, Health Affairs, July 18, 2006.

[5]Department of Agriculture. "Characteristics of Food Stamp Households: Fiscal Year 2003," Prepared by Karen Cunnygham (Mathematica Policy Research Inc.), November 2004.

[6]Council of Economic Advisers, "Immigration's Economic Impact," Washington, D.C. June 20, 2007.

[7]Arizona: http://udallcenter.arizona.edu/programs/immigration/publications/impact_judy.pdf California: http://www.labor.ca.gov/panel/impactimmcaecon.pdf Chicago: http://www.uic.edu/cuppa/uicued/npublications/recent/undoc_full.pdf Las Vegas: http://www.reviewjournal.com/lvrj_home/2003/Apr-17-Thu-2003/news/21129278.html Minnesota: http://www.auditor.leg.state.mn.us/Ped/pedrep/ecoimpact.pdf New York: http://www.fiscalpolicy.org/immigration2007.html North Carolina: http://www.kenan-flagler.unc.edu/assets/documents/2006_KenanInstituteHispanicStudy.pdf South Carolina: http://www.sph.sc.edu/cli/documents/CMAReport0809.pdf Texas: http://www.ailf.org/ipc/spotlight/spotlight_122206.pdf

[8]Center for Urban Economic Development, University of Illinois at Chicago. "Chicago's Undocumented Immigrants: An Analysis of Wages, Working Conditions, and Economic Contributions," Chirag Mehta, Nik Theodore, Iliana Mora & Jennifer Wade, February 2002. http://www.uic.edu/cuppa/uicued/Publications/RECENT/undoc_full.pdf

[9]Udall Center for Studies in Public Policy. The University of Arizona. "The Economic Impacts of Immigrants in Arizona," Judith Gans. July 2007.

[10]Office of the Comptroller, Texas. "Undocumented Immigrants in Texas:A Financial Anaylsis of the Impact to the State Budget and Economy." Special Report. Carole Keeton Strayhorn. December 2006.

[11]Council of Economic Advisers. Executive Office of the President. "Immigration's Economic Impact," Washington, D.C. June 20, 2007. http://www.whitehouse.gov/cea/cea_immigration_062007.html

[12]American Immigration Law Foundation. "Rethinking the Effects of Immigration on Wages: New Data and Analysis from 1990-2004," Giovanni Peri, October 2006. http://www.ailf.org/ipc/infocus/infocus_10306.pdf

[13]National Research Council, The New Americans:Economic, Demographic, and Fiscal Effects of Immigration, ed. James P. Smith and Barry Edmonston (Washington, D.C.:National Academy Press, 1997).

[14]Council of Economic Advisers. Executive Office of the President. "Immigration's Economic Impact," Washington, D.C. June 20, 2007. http://www.whitehouse.gov/cea/cea_immigration_062007.html

[15]Ibid Center for Research and Analysis of Migration (Department of Economics, University Date created: January 25, 2008 College London). "How Immigration Affects U.S. Cities," David Card (UC Berkeley), June 2007.

[16]Pew Hispanic Center. "Growth in the Foreign-Born Workforce and Employment of the Native Born," Rakesh Kochhar, August 10, 2006.

[17]Public Policy Institute of California. "How Immigrants Affect California Employment and Wages," Giovanni Peri. California Counts: Population Trends and Profiles. Volume 8, Number 3. February 2007.

[18]International Migration Policy Program of the Carnegie Endowment for International Peace and the Urban Institute. "Coming of Age in Immigrant America," Jan/Feb 1998.

[19]International Migration Policy Program of the Carnegie Endowment for International Peace and the Urban Institute. "Coming of Age in Immigrant America," Jan/Feb 1998. http://www.migrationpolicy.org/files/RPMVol1-No6.pdf

[20]Pew Hispanic Center. "English Usage Among Hispanics in United States," November 2007. http://pewhispanic.org/reports/report.php?ReportID=82

[22]Pew Hispanic Center. "English Usage Among Hispanics in United States," November 2007.

[23]Pew Hispanic Center. "English Usage Among Hispanics in United States," November 2007. http://pewhispanic.org/reports/report.php?ReportID=82

[24]Public Policy Institute of California. "Second-Generation Immigrants in California." Karthick Ramakrishnan and Hans P. Johnson. California Counts: Population Trends and Profiles.Vol. 6 No. 4 May 2005.

[24]National Association of Latino Elected Officials. Press release. February 1, 2007. http://www.naleo.org/pr020107.html

[25]Pew Hispanic Center. "Growing Share of Immigrants Choosing Naturalization." Jeffrey Passel. March 28, 2007.

[26]Washington Post. "Immigrant Paperwork Backs Up at DHS," Spenser S. Hsu. November 22, 2007.

[27]New York Times. "Legal Immigrants Facing a Longer Wait," Julia Preston. January 18, 2008.

[28]Testimony by Emilio Gonzalez, Director of U.S. Citizenship and Immigration Services for a Hearing before the House Judiciary Committee. January 17, 2008.

[29]SEIU. Press Release. Testimony by Eliseo Medina on Naturalization backlogs before the House Judiciary Committee. January 17, 2008.

[30]Economic Report of the President. Council of Economic Advisers. Washington D.C. 2005.

[31]Center for Urban Economic Development. University of Illinois at Chicago. "Chicago's Undocumented Immigrants: An Analysis of Wages, Working Conditions, and Economic Contributions,". Chirag Mehta Nik Theodore, Iliana Mora, Jennifer Wade. February 2002.

[32]Center for Urban Economic Development. University of Illinois at Chicago. "Chicago's Undocumented Immigrants: An Analysis of Wages, Working Conditions, and Economic Contributions,". Chirag Mehta Nik Theodore, Iliana Mora, Jennifer Wade. February 2002.

[33]The Community Foundation and the Urban Institute. "Civic Contributions: Taxes Paid by Immigrants in the Washington, DC, Metropolitan Area. Randy Capps, Everett Henderson, Jeffery Passel, Michael Fix. May 2006.

[34]Testimony of Patrick P. O'Carroll, Jr., Inspector General of the Social Security Administration, before the U.S. Senate, Committee on Finance, regarding "Administrative Challenges Facing the Social Security Administration," March 14, 2006.

[35]New York Times. "Illegal Immigrants Are a Bolstering Social Security With Billions," Eduardo Porter. (April 5, 2005).

[36]Pew Hispanic Center. "Between Here and There: How Attached Are Latino Immigrants To Date created: January 25, 2008 Their Native Country?" Roger Waldinger (UCLA), October 25, 2007. http://pewhispanic.org/files/reports/80.pdf

[37]National Immigration Forum & Cato Institute: A Fiscal Portrait of the Newest Americans," Stephen Moore, 1998. http://www.eric.ed.gov/ERICDocs/data/ericdocs2sql/content_storage_01/0000019b/80/17/4a/04.pdf

[38]Russell Sage Foundation. "Immigrants and Boomers: Forging a New Social Contract for the Future of America," Dowell Myers, 2007.

[39]Harvard University Joint Center for Housing Studies. "New Americans, New Homeowners: The Role and Relevance of Foreign-Born First-Time

Homebuyers in the U.S. Housing Market," Rachel Borgadus Drew, August, 2002.

[40]"Buying into the American Dream? Mexican Immigrants, Legal Status and Homeownership in Los Angeles County," Eileen Diaz McConnell and Enrico A. Marcelli. Social Science Quarterly. Vol. 8, No. 1. March 2007.

[41]Ibid.

[42]National Institute of Justice, an agency of the U.S. Department of Justice. "On Immigration and Crime," Ramiro Martinez, Jr., and Matthew T. Lee, July 2000. http://www.ncjrs.org/criminal_justice2000/vol_1/02j.pdf

[43]American Immigration Law Foundation. "The Myth of Immigrant Criminality and the Paradox of Assimilation: Incarceration Rates among Native and Foreign-Born Men," Rubén G. Rumbaut and Walter A. Ewing, Spring 2007. http://www.ailf.org/ipc/special_report/sr_022107.pdf)

[44]National Bureau of Economic Research. Working Paper Series. "Why are Immigrants' Incarceration Rayes so Low? Evidence of Selective Immigration, Deterence, and Deportation." Kritine F. Butcher and Anne Morrison Piehl. July 2007.

[45]Zogby International. "Greater Hazleton Area Civic Partnership," Michael Colgero, et al. August 2007.

[46]Pew Hispanic Center. "Size and Characteristics of the Unauthorized Migrant Population in the U.S." Jeffrey S. Passel, March 2006.

[47]Pew Hispanic Center. "Modes of Entry for the Unauthorized Migrant Population." Fact Sheet. May 2006. http://pewhispanic.org/factsheets/factsheet.php?FactsheetID=19

[48]Cato Institute. "Backfire at the Border: Why Enforcement Without Legalization Cannot Stop Illegal Immigration," Douglas Massey, June 2005. http://www.freetrade.org/pubs/pas/tpa-029.pdf

[49]Ibid

[50]Congressional Research Services. "Border Security: Barriers Along the U.S International Border," Blas Nunez-Neto and Stephen Vina, December 2006. http://www.stormingmedia.us/23/2319/A231954.html Date created: January 25, 2008

Questions

1. How many immigrants come to the United States every year?
2. How many of them are illegal?
3. How many of them are Latino?
4. What sorts of contributions do immigrants make to American society?
5. What social and economic costs are related to immigration?

Two Ways to Belong in America

Bharati Mukherjee

Bharati Mukherjee was born in Calcutta, India in 1940. At age eight she moved to Europe with her family, where she spent the next three and a half years. After her college education in Calcutta, she went to the United States and the University of Iowa, earning an M.F.A. in writing in 1963 and a Ph.D. in English and Comparative Literature in 1969. It was at Iowa that she met and married a Canadian student from Harvard and eventually left the U.S. to live in Montreal and Toronto with him. In 1972's The Tiger's Daughter, *she tells the story of a girl who returns to India after years of being away only to confront the continued poverty and intense discrimination against women in that country. The novel reflects one of Mukherjee's ongoing thematic interests. Her novel* Wife *(1975) deals directly and powerfully with the treatment of women and female identity. The treatment of women in Indian culture and the struggles of immigrants received further attention in* An Invisible Woman *(1981) and* Darkness *(1985). For* The Middleman and Other Stories *(1988), Mukherjee received the National Book Critics Circle Award. These stories deal with the experiences of Indian people living in Canada and the U.S.* Jasmine *(1989) relates the story of a young Indian woman who is widowed at seventeen. To escape the brutal experience of that country, such as rape and other forms of objectification, she goes to the United States only to confront loneliness and be subjected to racism. In* The Holder of the World *(1993), the main character struggles to become free from the bonds of relationships with men.* Leave It to Me *(1997) is about an abandoned child who seeks revenge on the parents who left her at an orphanage.* Desirable Daughters *(2002) is a story about a pre-arranged marriage gone wrong.* The Tree Bride *(2004), the sequel to* Daughters, *shows a woman in the midst of the turmoil of assimilation and her efforts to come to terms with the past. Currently, she teaches English at the University of California, Berkeley. In the following selection from the Op-Ed section of the* New York Times, *Mukherjee explores different ideas of immigration and assimilation through a personal account of her relationship with her sister.*

1 This is a tale of two sisters from Calcutta, Mira and Bharati, who have lived in the United States for some 35 years, but who find themselves on different sides in the current debate over the status of immigrants. 1

I am an American citizen and she is not. I am moved that thousands of long-term residents are finally taking the oath of citizenship. She is not.

Mira arrived in Detroit in 1960 to study child psychology and pre-school education. I followed her a year later to study creative writing at the University of Iowa. When we left India, we were almost identical in appearance and attitude. We dressed alike, in saris; we expressed identical views on politics, social issues, love and marriage in the same Calcutta convent-school accent. We would endure our two years in America, secure our degrees, then return to India to marry the grooms of our father's choosing.

Instead, Mira married an Indian student in 1962 who was getting his business administration degree at Wayne State University. They soon acquired the labor certifications necessary for the green card of hassle-free residence and employment.

5 Mira still lives in Detroit, works in the Southfield, Mich., school system, and has become nationally recognized for her contributions in the fields of pre-school education and parent-teacher relationships. After 36 years as a legal immigrant in this country, she clings passionately to her Indian citizenship and hopes to go home to India when she retires. 5

In Iowa City in 1963, I married a fellow student, an American of Canadian parentage. Because of the accident of his North Dakota birth, I bypassed labor-certification requirements and the race-related "quota" system that favored the applicant's country of origin over his or her merit. I was prepared for (and even welcomed) the emotional strain that came with marrying outside my ethnic community. In 33 years of marriage, we have lived in every part of North America. By choosing a husband who was not my father's selection, I was opting for fluidity, self-invention, blue jeans and T-shirts, and renouncing 3,000 years (at least) of caste-observant, "pure culture" marriage in the Mukherjee family. My books have often been read as unapologetic (and in some quarters overenthusiastic) texts for cultural and psychological "mongrelization." It's a word I celebrate.

Mira and I have stayed sisterly close by phone. In our regular Sunday morning conversations, we are unguardedly affectionate. I am her only blood relative on this continent. We expect to see each other through the looming crises of aging and ill health without being asked. Long before Vice President Gore's "Citizenship U.S.A." drive, we'd had our polite arguments over the ethics of retaining an overseas citizenship while expecting the permanent protection and economic benefits that come with living and working in America.

Like well-raised sisters, we never said what was really on our minds, but we probably pitied one another. She, for the lack of structure in my life, the erasure of Indianness, the absence of an unvarying daily core. I, for the narrowness of her perspective, her uninvolvement with the mythic depths or the superficial pop culture of this society. But, now, with the scapegoating of "aliens" (documented or illegal) on the increase, and the targeting of long-term legal immigrants like Mira for new scrutiny and new self-consciousness, she and I find ourselves unable to maintain the same polite discretion. We were always unacknowledged adversaries, and we are now, more than ever, sisters.

"I feel used," Mira raged on the phone the other night. "I feel manipulated and discarded. This is such an unfair way to treat a person who was invited to stay and work here because of her talent. My employer went to the I.N.S. and petitioned for the labor certification. For over 30 years, I've invested my creativity and professional skills into the improvement of this country's pre-school system. I've obeyed all the rules, I've paid my taxes, I love my work, I love my students, I love the friends I've made. How dare America now change its rules in midstream? If America wants to make new rules curtailing benefits of legal immigrants, they should apply only to immigrants who arrive after those rules are already in place." To my ears, it sounded like the description of a long-enduring, comfortable yet loveless marriage, without risk or recklessness. Have we the right to demand, and to expect, that we be loved? (That, to me, is the subtext of the arguments by immigration advocates.) My sister is an expatriate, professionally generous and creative, socially courteous and gracious, and that's as far as her Americanization can go. She is here to maintain an identity, not to transform it.

I asked her if she would follow the example of others who have
10 decided to become citizens because of the anti-immigration bills in Congress. And here, she surprised me. "If America wants to play the manipulative game, I'll play it too," she snapped. "I'll become a U.S. citizen for now, then change back to Indian when I'm ready to go home. I feel some kind of irrational attachment to India that I don't to America. Until all this hysteria against legal immigrants, I was totally happy. Having my green card meant I could visit any place in the world I wanted to and then come back to a job that's satisfying and that I do very well."

In one family, from two sisters alike as peas in a pod, there could not be a wider divergence of immigrant experience. America spoke to me—I married it—I embraced the demotion from expatriate aristocrat to immigrant nobody, surrendering those thousands of years of "pure culture," the saris, the delightfully accented English. She retained them all. Which of us is the freak?

Mira's voice, I realize, is the voice not just of the immigrant South Asian community but of an immigrant community of the millions who have stayed rooted in one job, one city, one house, one ancestral culture, one cuisine, for the entirety of their productive years. She speaks for greater numbers than I possibly can. Only the fluency of her English and the anger, rather than fear, born of confidence from her education, differentiate her from the seamstresses, the domestics, the technicians, the shop owners, the millions of hard-working but effectively silenced documented immigrants as well as their less fortunate "illegal" brothers and sisters.

Nearly 20 years ago, when I was living in my husband's ancestral homeland of Canada, I was always well-employed but never allowed to feel part of the local Quebec or larger Canadian society. Then, through a Green Paper that invited a national referendum on the unwanted side effects of "nontraditional" immigration, the Government officially turned against its immigrant communities, particularly those from South Asia.

I felt then the same sense of betrayal that Mira feels now. I will never forget the pain of that sudden turning, and the casual racist outbursts the Green Paper elicited. That sense of betrayal had its desired effect and drove me, and thousands like me, from the country.

Mira and I differ, however, in the ways in which we hope to interact with the country that we have chosen to live in. She is happier to live in America as expatriate Indian than as an immigrant American. I need to feel like a part of the community I have adopted (as I tried to feel in Canada as well). I need to put roots down, to vote and make the difference that I can. The price that the immigrant willingly pays, and that the exile avoids, is the trauma of self-transformation.

Critical Thinking and Reading

From Chapter 8 of *LB Brief: The Little, Brown Handbook, Brief Version,* Fourth Edition. Jane E. Aaron.

Critical Thinking and Reading

Why and how should I think and read critically?

Throughout college and beyond, you will be expected to think and read critically—that is, to question, test, and build on what others say and what you yourself think. In daily life, critical thinking helps you figure out why things happen to you or what your experiences mean. In school and at work, critical thinking sharpens your ability to learn and to perform. It helps you understand which ideas are useful, fair, and wise—and which are not.

a Use techniques of critical reading.

In college and work, much of your critical thinking will focus on written texts (a short story, a journal article, a blog) or on visual objects (a photograph, a chart, a film). Like all subjects worthy of critical consideration, such works operate on at least three levels: (1) what the creator actually says or shows, (2) what the creator does not say or show but builds into the work (intentionally or not), and (3) what you think. Discovering each level of the work, even if it is visual, involves four main steps: previewing the material, reading actively, summarizing, and forming a critical response.

CULTURE LANGUAGE The idea of reading critically may require you to make some adjustments if readers in your native culture tend to seek understanding or agreement more than engagement in what they read. Readers of English use texts for all kinds of reasons, including pleasure, reinforcement, and information. But they also read skeptically, critically, to see the author's motives, test their own ideas, and arrive at new knowledge.

1 ■ Previewing the material

When you're reading a work of literature, such as a short story or a poem, it's often best just to plunge right in. But for critical reading of other works, it's worthwhile to skim before reading word for word, forming expectations and even some preliminary questions. The preview will make your reading more informed and fruitful.

mycomplab

Visit *mycomplab.com* for more resources and exercises on critical thinking and reading.

- **Gauge length and level.** Is the material brief and straightforward so that you can read it in one sitting, or does it require more time?
- **Check the facts of publication.** Does the date of publication suggest currency or datedness? Does the publisher or publication specialize in scholarly articles, popular books, or something else? For a Web publication, who or what sponsors the site—an individual? a nonprofit organization? a government body? a college or university?
- **Look for content cues.** What do the title, introduction, headings, illustrations, conclusion, and other features tell you about the topic, the author's approach, and the main ideas?
- **Learn about the author.** Does a biography tell you about the author's publications, interests, biases, and reputation in the field? If there is no biography, what can you gather about the author from his or her words? Use a Web search to trace unfamiliar authors.
- **Consider your preliminary response.** What do you already know about the topic? What questions do you have about either the topic or the author's approach to it? What biases of your own—for instance, curiosity, boredom, or an outlook similar or opposed to the author—might influence your reading of the work?

Exercise 1 Previewing an essay

Following is an essay by Thomas Sowell, an economist, newspaper columnist, and author of many books on economics, politics, and education. The essay was first published in the 1990s, but its subject remains current. Preview the essay using the preceding guidelines, and then read it once or twice, until you think you understand what the author is saying. Note your questions and reactions in writing.

Student Loans

The first lesson of economics is scarcity: There is never enough of anything to fully satisfy all those who want it. 1

The first lesson of politics is to disregard the first lesson of economics. When politicians discover some group that is being vocal about not having as much as they want, the "solution" is to give them more. Where do politicians get this "more"? They rob Peter to pay Paul. 2

After a while, of course, they discover that Peter doesn't have enough. Bursting with compassion, politicians rush to the rescue. Needless to say, they do not admit that robbing Peter to pay Paul was a dumb idea in the first place. On the contrary, they now rob Tom, Dick, and Harry to help Peter. 3

The latest chapter in this long-running saga is that politicians have now suddenly discovered that many college students graduate heavily in debt. To politicians it follows, as the night follows the day, that the government should come to their rescue with the taxpayers' money. 4

How big is this crushing burden of college students' debt that we 5
hear so much about from politicians and media deep thinkers? For those students who graduate from public colleges owing money, the debt averages a little under $7000. For those who graduate from private colleges owing money, the average debt is a little under $9000.

Buying a very modestly priced automobile involves more debt than 6
that. And a car loan has to be paid off faster than the ten years that college graduates get to repay their student loans. Moreover, you have to keep buying cars every several years, while one college education lasts a lifetime.

College graduates of course earn higher incomes than other peo- 7
ple. Why, then, should we panic at the thought that they have to repay loans for the education which gave them their opportunities? Even graduates with relatively modest incomes pay less than 10 percent of their annual salary on the loan the first year—with declining percentages in future years, as their pay increases.

Political hysteria and media hype may focus on the low-income stu- 8
dent with a huge debt. That is where you get your heart-rending stories—even if they are not all that typical. In reality, the soaring student loans of the past decade have resulted from allowing high-income people to borrow under government programs.

Before 1978, college loans were available through government pro- 9
grams only to students whose family income was below some cut-off level. That cut-off level was about double the national average income, but at least it kept out the Rockefellers and the Vanderbilts. But, in an era of "compassion," Congress took off even those limits.

That opened the floodgates. No matter how rich you were, it still 10
paid to borrow money through the government at low interest rates. The money you had set aside for your children's education could be invested somewhere else, at higher interest rates. Then, when the student loan became due, parents could pay it off with the money they had set aside—pocketing the difference in interest rates.

To politicians and the media, however, the rapidly growing loans 11
showed what a great "need" there was. The fact that many students welshed when time came to repay their loans showed how "crushing" their burden of debt must be. In reality, those who welsh typically have smaller loans, but have dropped out of college before finishing. People who are irresponsible in one way are often irresponsible in other ways.

No small amount of the deterioration of college standards has been 12
due to the increasingly easy availability of college to people who are not very serious about getting an education. College is not a bad place to hang out for a few years, if you have nothing better to do, and if someone else is paying for it. Its costs are staggering, but the taxpayers carry much of that burden, not only for state universities and city colleges, but also to an increasing extent even for "private" institutions.

Numerous government subsidies and loan programs make it possible 13
for many people to use vast amounts of society's resources at low cost to themselves. Whether in money terms or in real terms, federal aid to higher education has increased several hundred percent since 1970. That has en-

> abled colleges to raise their tuition by leaps and bounds and enabled professors to be paid more and more for doing less and less teaching.
>
> Naturally all these beneficiaries are going to create hype and hyste- 14
> ria to keep more of the taxpayers' money coming in. But we would be fools to keep on writing blank checks for them.
>
> When you weigh the cost of things, in economics that's called 15
> "trade-offs." In politics, it's called "mean-spirited." Apparently, if we just took a different attitude, scarcity would go away.
>
> —Thomas Sowell

2 ▪ Reading

Reading is itself more than a one-step process. You want to understand the first level on which the text operates—what the author actually says—and begin to form your impressions.

First reading

The first time through new material, read as steadily and smoothly as possible, trying to get the gist of what the author is saying.

- **Read in a place where you can concentrate.** Choose a quiet environment away from distractions such as music or talking.
- **Give yourself time.** Rushing yourself or worrying about something else you have to do will prevent you from grasping what you read.
- **Try to enjoy the work.** Seek connections between it and what you already know. Appreciate new information, interesting relationships, forceful writing, humor, good examples.
- **Make notes sparingly during this first reading.** Mark major stumbling blocks—such as a paragraph you don't understand—so that you can try to resolve them before rereading.

CULTURE LANGUAGE If English is not your first language and you come across unfamiliar words during a first reading, don't look them up until you are finished. Stopping while reading can distract you from seeing the author's overall meaning. Instead, try to guess the meanings of unfamiliar words from their contexts, circle them, and look them up later.

Rereading

After the first reading, plan on at least one other. This time read *slowly.* Your main concern should be to grasp the content and how it is constructed. That means rereading a paragraph if you didn't get the point or using a dictionary to look up words you don't know.

Use your pen, pencil, or keyboard freely to highlight and distill the text:

- **Distinguish main ideas from supporting ideas.** Look for the central idea, or thesis, for the main idea of each paragraph or section, and for the evidence supporting ideas.
- **Learn key terms.** Understand both their meanings and their applications.
- **Discern the connections among ideas.** Be sure you see why the author moves from point A to point B to point C and how those points relate to support the central idea. It often helps to outline the text or to summarize it (see opposite).
- **Distinguish between facts and opinions.** Especially when reading an argument, tease apart the facts from the author's opinions that may or may not be based on facts.
- **Add your own comments.** In the margins or separately, note links to other readings or to class discussions, questions to explore further, possible topics for your writing, points you find especially strong or weak.

An example of critical reading

The following samples show how a student, Charlene Robinson, approached "Student Loans." After her first reading, Robinson went through Sowell's text more slowly and added her comments and questions. Here are the first four paragraphs with her annotations:

> The first lesson of economics is scarcity: There is never enough of anything to fully satisfy all those who want it. *fact*
>
> The first lesson of politics is to disregard the first lesson of economics. When politicians discover some group that is being vocal about not having as much as they want, the "solution" is to give them more. Where do politicians get this "more"? They rob Peter to pay Paul. *opinion—basic contradiction between economics and politics* ← *biblical reference?*
>
> After a while, of course, they discover that Peter doesn't have enough. Bursting with compassion, politicians rush to the rescue. Needless to say, they do not admit that robbing Peter to pay Paul was a dumb idea in the first place. On the contrary, they now rob Tom, Dick, and Harry to help Peter. *ironic and dismissive language*
>
> The latest chapter in this long-running saga is that politicians have now suddenly discovered that many college students graduate heavily in debt. To politicians it follows, as the night follows the day, that the government should come to their rescue with the taxpayers' money. *politicians = fools? or irresponsible?*

After reading the text, Robinson wrote about it in the journal she kept on her computer. She divided the journal into two columns, one each for the text and her responses. Here is the portion pertaining to the paragraphs above:

Text	Responses
Economics teaches lessons (1), and politics (politicians) and economics are at odds.	Is economics truer or more reliable than politics? More scientific?
Politicians don't accept econ. limits—always trying to satisfy "vocal" voters by giving them more of what they want (2).	Politicians do spend tax money, but do they always disregard economics? Evidence?
"Robbing Peter to pay Paul" (2)—the Bible (the Apostles)?	
Politicians support student-loan program with taxpayer refunds bec. of "vocal" voters (2-4): another ex. of not accepting econ. limits.	I support the loan program, too. Are politicians being irresponsible when they do? (Dismissive language underlined on copy.)

You should try to answer the questions about meaning that you raise in your annotations and your journal, and that may take another reading or some digging in other sources, such as dictionaries and encyclopedias. Recording in your journal what you think the author means will help you build an understanding of the text, and a focused attempt to summarize will help even more (see below). Such efforts will resolve any confusion you feel, or they will give you the confidence to say that your confusion is the fault of the author, not the reader.

Exercise 2 **Reading**

Read Sowell's essay earlier in this chapter at least twice, until you think you understand what the author is saying. Either on these pages or separately, note your questions and reactions in writing, as student writer Charlene Robinson did for the first four paragraphs. Look up any words you don't know, and try to answer your questions. You might want to discuss the essay with your classmates as well.

3 ▪ Summarizing

A good way to master the content of a text and to see its strengths and weaknesses is to **summarize** it: distill it to its main points, in your own words. The following box gives a method of summarizing:

Writing a summary

- **Understand the meaning.** Look up words or concepts you don't know so that you understand the author's sentences and how they relate to one another.
- **Understand the organization.** Work through the text to identify its sections—single paragraphs or groups of paragraphs focused on a single topic. To understand how parts of a work relate to one another, try drawing a tree diagram or creating an outline.

(continued)

Writing a summary

(continued)

- **Distill each section.** Write a one- or two-sentence summary of each section you identify. Focus on the main point of the section, omitting examples, facts, and other supporting evidence.
- **State the main idea.** Write a sentence or two capturing the author's central idea.
- **Support the main idea.** Write a full paragraph (or more, if needed) that begins with the central idea and supports it with the sentences that summarize sections of the work. The paragraph should concisely and accurately state the thrust of the entire work.
- ***Use your own words.*** By writing, you re-create the meaning of the work in a way that makes sense for you.

Summarizing even a passage of text can be tricky. Below is one attempt to summarize the following material from an introductory biology textbook.

Original text

As astronomers study newly discovered planets orbiting distant stars, they hope to find evidence of water on these far-off celestial bodies, for water is the substance that makes possible life as we know it here on Earth. All organisms familiar to us are made mostly of water and live in an environment dominated by water. They require water more than any other substance. Human beings, for example, can survive for quite a few weeks without food, but only a week or so without water. Molecules of water participate in many chemical reactions necessary to sustain life. Most cells are surrounded by water, and cells themselves are about 70–95% water. Three-quarters of Earth's surface is submerged in water. Although most of this water is in liquid form, water is also present on Earth as ice and vapor. Water is the only common substance to exist in the natural environment in all three physical states of matter: solid, liquid, and gas.

—Neil A. Campbell and Jane B. Reece, *Biology*

Draft summary

Astronomers look for water in outer space because life depends on it. It is the most common substance on Earth and in living cells, and it can be a liquid, a solid (ice), or a gas (vapor).

This summary accurately restates ideas in the original, but it does not pare the passage to its essence. The work of astronomers and the three physical states of water add color and texture to the original, but they are asides to the key concept that water sustains life because of its role in life. The following revision narrows the summary to this concept:

Revised summary

Water is the most essential support for life, the dominant substance on Earth and in living cells and a component of life-sustaining chemical processes.

When Charlene Robinson summarized Thomas Sowell's "Student Loans," she first drafted this sentence about paragraphs 1–4:

Draft summary

As much as politicians would like to satisfy voters by giving them everything they ask for, the government cannot afford a student loan program.

Reading the sentence and Sowell's paragraphs, Robinson saw that this draft misread the text by asserting that the government cannot afford student loans. She realized that Sowell's point is more complicated than that and rewrote her summary:

Revised summary

As their support of the government's student loan program illustrates, politicians ignore the economic reality that using resources to benefit one group (students in debt) involves taking the resources from another group (taxpayers).

Notes Using your own words when writing a summary not only helps you understand the meaning but also constitutes the first step in avoiding plagiarism. The second step is to cite the source when you use it in something written for others.

Do not count on the AutoSummarize function on your word processor for summarizing texts that you may have copied onto your computer. The summaries are rarely accurate, and you will not gain the experience of interacting with the texts on your own.

Exercise 3 Summarizing

Start where the preceding summary of Thomas Sowell's essay ends (at paragraph 5) to summarize the entire essay. Your summary, in your own words, should not exceed one paragraph.

b Form a critical response.

Once you've grasped the content of what you're reading—what the author says—then you can turn to understanding what the author does not say outright but suggests or implies or even lets slip. At this stage you are concerned with the purpose or intention of the author and with how he or she carries it out.

Critical thinking and reading consist of four overlapping operations: analyzing, interpreting, synthesizing, and (often) evaluating.

Analyzing

Analysis is the separation of something into its parts or elements, the better to understand it. To see these elements in what you are reading, begin with a question that reflects your purpose in analyzing the text: why you're curious about it or what you're trying to make out of it. This question will serve as a kind of lens that highlights some features and not others.

Analyzing Thomas Sowell's "Student Loans," you might ask one of these questions:

Questions for analysis	Elements
What is Sowell's attitude toward politicians?	References to politicians: content, words, tone
How does Sowell support assertions about the loan program's costs?	Support: evidence, such as statistics and examples

Interpreting

Identifying the elements of something is only the beginning: you also need to interpret the meaning or significance of the elements and of the whole. Interpretation usually requires you to infer the author's **assumptions**—that is, opinions or beliefs about what is or what could or should be. (*Infer* means to draw a conclusion based on evidence.)

Assumptions are pervasive: we all adhere to certain values, beliefs, and opinions. But assumptions are not always stated outright. Speakers and writers may judge that their audience already understands and accepts their assumptions; they may not even be aware of their assumptions; or they may deliberately refrain from stating their assumptions for fear that the audience will disagree. That is why your job as a critical thinker is to interpret what the assumptions are.

Thomas Sowell's "Student Loans" is based on certain assumptions, some obvious, some not. If you were analyzing Sowell's attitude toward politicians, as suggested earlier, you would focus on his statements about them. Sowell says that they "disregard the first lesson of economics" (paragraph 2), which implies that they ignore important principles (knowing that Sowell is an economist himself makes this a reasonable assumption on your part). Sowell also says that politicians "rob Peter to pay Paul," are "[b]ursting with compassion," "do not admit . . . a dumb idea," are characters in a "long-running saga," and arrive at the solution of spending taxes "as the night follows the day"—that is, inevitably (paragraphs 2–4). From these statements and others, you can infer the following:

> Sowell assumes that politicians become compassionate when a cause is loud and popular, not necessarily just, and they act irresponsibly by trying to solve the problem with other people's (taxpayers') money.

Synthesizing

If you stopped at analysis and interpretation, critical thinking and reading might leave you with a pile of elements and possible meanings but no vision of the whole. With **synthesis** you make connections among parts *or* among wholes. You use your perspective—your knowledge and beliefs—to create a new whole by drawing conclusions about relationships and implications.

Synthesis is a key component of academic reading and writing. Sometimes you'll respond directly to a text, as in the following statement about Thomas Sowell's essay "Student Loans," which connects Sowell's assumptions about politicians to a larger idea also implied by the essay:

> Sowell's view that politicians are irresponsible with taxpayers' money reflects his overall opinion that the laws of economics, not politics, should drive government.

Often synthesis will take you outside the text to the surroundings. The following questions can help you investigate the context of a work:

- **How does the work compare with works by others?** For instance, how have other writers responded to Sowell's views on student loans?
- **How does the work fit into the context of other works by the same author or group?** How do Sowell's views on student loans typify, or not, the author's other writing on political and economic issues?
- **What cultural, economic, or political forces influence the work?** What other examples might Sowell have given to illustrate his view that economics, not politics, should determine government spending?
- **What historical forces influence the work?** How has the indebtedness of college students changed over the past four decades?

Evaluating

Critical reading and writing often end at synthesis: you form and explain your understanding of what the work says and doesn't say. If you are also expected to **evaluate** the work, however, you will go further to judge its quality and significance. You may be evaluating a source you've discovered in research, or you may be completing an assignment to state and defend a judgment, a statement such as *Thomas Sowell does not summon the evidence to support his case.* You can read Charlene Robinson's critical analysis of Thomas Sowell's "Student Loans."

Evaluation takes a certain amount of confidence. You may think that you lack the expertise to cast judgment on another's work, especially if the work is difficult or the author well known. True, the more informed you are, the better a critical reader you are. But conscientious reading and analysis will give you the internal authority to judge a work *as it stands* and *as it seems to you,* against your own unique bundle of experiences, observations, and attitudes.

Exercise 4 Reading an essay critically

Reread Thomas Sowell's "Student Loans" to form your own critical response to it. Focus on any elements suggested by your questions about the text: possibilities are assumptions, evidence, organization, use of language, tone, vision of education or students. Be sure to write while reading and thinking; your notes will help your analysis and enhance your creativity, and they will be essential for writing about the selection.

c View images critically.

Every day we are bombarded with images—pictures on billboards, commercials on television, graphs and charts in newspapers and textbooks, to name just a few examples. Most images slide by without our noticing them, or so we think. But images, sometimes even more than text, can influence us covertly. Their creators have purposes, some worthy, some not, and understanding those purposes requires critical reading. The method parallels that in the previous section for reading text critically: preview, read for comprehension, analyze, interpret, synthesize, and (often) evaluate.

1 ▪ Previewing an image

Your first step in exploring an image is to form initial impressions of the work's origin and purpose and to note distinctive features. This previewing process is like the one for previewing a text:

- **What do you see?** What is most striking about the image? What is its subject? What is the gist of any text or symbols? What is the overall effect of the image?
- **What are the facts of publication?** Where did you first see the image? Do you think the image was created especially for that location or for others as well? What can you tell about when the image was created?
- **What do you know about the person or group that created the image?** For instance, was the creator an artist, scholar, news organization, or corporation? What seems to have been the creator's purpose?
- **What is your preliminary response?** What about the image interests, confuses, or disturbs you? Are the form, style, and subject familiar or unfamiliar? How might your knowledge, experiences, and values influence your reception of the image?

If possible, print a copy of the image or scan it into your reading journal, and write comments in the image margins or separately.

2 ▪ Reading an image

Reading an image requires the same level of concentration as reading a text. The illustration below shows the notes that a student, Matthew Greene, made while reading an advertisement.

Try to answer the following questions about the image. If some answers aren't clear at this point, skip the question until later.

- **What is the purpose of the image?** Is it mainly explanatory, conveying information, or is it argumentative, trying to convince readers of something or persuade them to act? What information or point of view does it seem intended to get across?
- **Who is the intended audience for the image?** What does the source of the image, including its publication facts, tell about the image creator's expectations for readers' knowledge, interests,

Annotation of an image

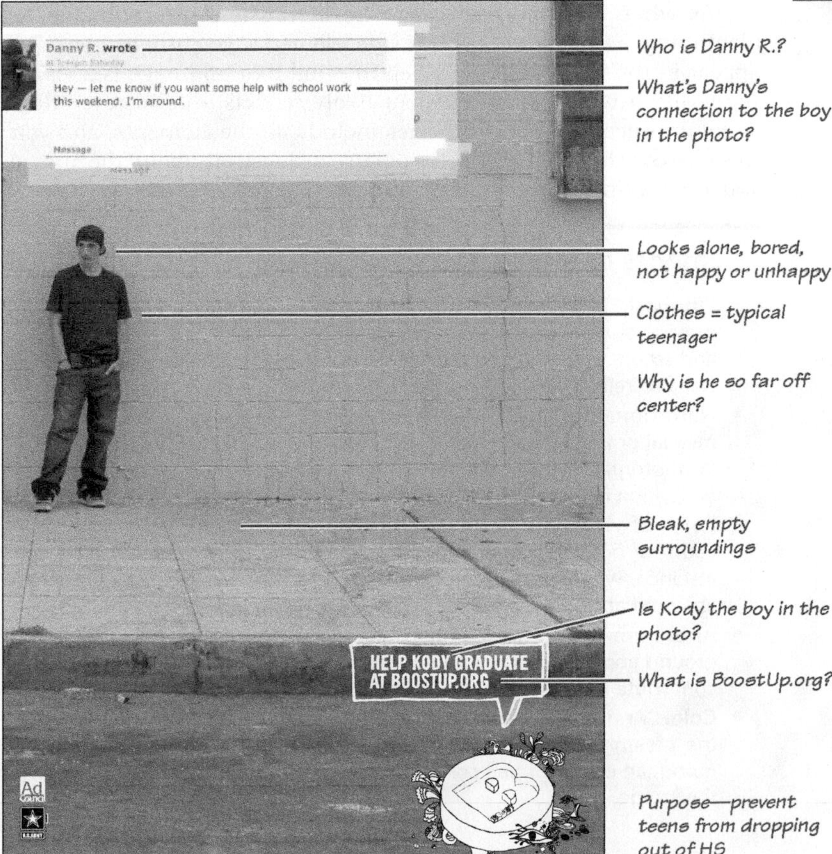

Advertisement for *BoostUp.org,* 2007

and attitudes? What do the features of the image itself add to your impression?

- **What do any words or symbols add to the image?** Whether located on the image or outside it (such as in a caption), do words or symbols add information, focus your attention, or alter your impression of the image?
- **What people, places, things, or action does the image show?** Does the image tell a story? Do its characters or other features tap into your knowledge, or are they unfamiliar?
- **What is the form of the image?** Is it a photograph, advertisement, painting, graph, diagram, cartoon, or something else? How do its content and apparent purpose and audience relate to its form?

3 ▪ Analyzing an image

Elements for analysis

As when analyzing a written work, you analyze an image by identifying its elements. The image elements you might consider appear in the following box. Keep in mind that an image is a visual *composition* whose every element likely reflects a deliberate effort to communicate. Still, few images include all the elements, and you can narrow the list further by posing a question about the image you are reading, as illustrated on the next page.

Elements of images

- **Emphasis:** Most images pull your eyes to certain features: a graph line moving sharply upward, a provocative figure, bright color, thick lines, and so on. The cropping of a photograph or the date range in a chart will also reflect what the image creator considers important.
- **Narration:** Most images tell stories, whether in a sequence (a TV commercial or a graph showing changes over time) or at a single moment (a photograph, a painting, or a pie chart). Sometimes dialog or a title or caption contributes to the story.
- **Point of view:** The image creator influences responses by taking account of both the viewer's physical relation to the image subject—for instance, whether it is seen head-on or from above—and the viewer's assumed attitude toward the subject.
- **Arrangement:** Patterns among colors or forms, figures in the foreground and background, and elements that are juxtaposed or set apart contribute to the image's meaning and effect.
- **Color:** An image's colors can direct the viewer's attention and convey the creator's attitude toward the subject. Color may also suggest a mood, an era, a cultural connection, or another frame in which to view the image.

- **Characterization:** The figures and objects in an image have certain qualities—sympathetic or not, desirable or not, and so on. Their characteristics reflect the roles they play in the image's story.
- **Context:** The source of an image or the background in an image affects its meaning, whether it is a graph from a scholarly journal or a photo of a car on a sunny beach.
- **Tension:** Images often communicate a problem or seize attention with features that seem wrong, such as misspelled or misaligned words, distorted figures, or controversial relations between characters.
- **Allusions:** An **allusion** is a reference to something the audience is likely to recognize and respond to. Examples include a cultural symbol such as a dollar sign, a mythological figure such as a unicorn, or a familiar movie character such as Darth Vader from *Star Wars*.

Question for analysis

You can focus your analysis of elements by framing your main interest in the image as a question. Matthew Greene posed this question about the *BoostUp.org* ad: *Does the ad move readers to learn more about* BoostUp.org *and how they can help teens to graduate?* The question led Greene to focus on certain elements of the ad:

Image elements	**Responses**
Emphasis	The ad's emptiness and placement of Kody at the far left puts primary emphasis on the boy's isolation. Danny R.'s message receives secondary emphasis.
Narration	The taped-on message suggests a story and connection between Kody and Danny R. Danny R. might be a friend, relative, or mentor. Based on the direct appeal in the word bubble at the bottom, it appears that Danny R. is trying to help Kody graduate by offering to help him with schoolwork.
Arrangement	The ad places Danny R. and Kody together on the left side of the page, with Danny's message a bright spot on the dull landscape. The appeal to help Kody graduate is subtle and set on its own—the last thing readers look at. It also pulls the elements together so that the ad makes sense.
Characterization	Kody is a sympathetic figure, a lonely-looking teen who would probably benefit from the help Danny R. is offering through *BoostUp.org*.

Sample image for analysis

The following image gives you a chance to analyze elements of a photograph. Try to answer the questions in the annotations.

Elements in a photograph

Emphasis: What is the focus of the photograph? What are your eyes drawn to?

Characterization: What does the man seem to be feeling? Consider especially his mouth and eyes.

Narration: What story or stories might the photograph tell?

Arrangement: What is interesting about the arrangement of elements?

Color: The photograph was created in black and white. What does this presentation contribute to the image? How might the image differ in full color?

Allusion: What symbol do you see? What meaning does it give to the photograph?

Photograph by Steve Simon

4 ▪ Interpreting an image

The strategies for interpreting an image parallel those for interpreting a written text. In this process you look more deeply at the elements, considering them in relation to the image creator's likely assumptions and intentions. You aim to draw reasonable inferences about the image creator's assumptions to explain *why* the image looks as it does. Consider this inference about the *BoostUp.org* advertisement:

> The creators of the *BoostUp.org* ad assume that readers want students to graduate from high school.

This statement is supported by the ad's text: the word bubble connecting to the *BoostUp.org* logo specifically says, "Help Kody graduate at *BoostUp.org*."

5 ▪ Synthesizing ideas about an image

With synthesis you take analysis and interpretation a step further to consider how a work's elements and underlying assumptions relate and what the overall message is. You may also expand your synthesis to view the whole image in a larger context: How does the work fit into the context of other works? What cultural, economic, political, or historical forces influence the work?

Placing an image in its context often requires research. For instance, to learn more about the assumptions underlying the *BoostUp.org* advertisement and the goals of the larger ad campaign, Matthew Greene visited the Web sites of *BoostUp.org* and the Ad Council, one of the ad's sponsors. The following entry from his reading journal synthesizes this research and his own ideas about the ad:

> The *BoostUp.org* magazine ad that features Kody is part of a larger campaign designed to raise public awareness about high school dropouts and encourage pubic support to help teens stay in school. Sponsored by the US Army and the nonprofit Ad Council, *BoostUp.org* profiles high school seniors who are at risk of dropping out and asks individuals to write the students personal messages of support. Ads like "Kody" are the first point of contact between the public and the teens, but they don't by themselves actually help the teens. For that, readers need to visit *BoostUp.org*. Thus the ad's elements work together like pieces of a puzzle, with the solution to be found only on the Web site.

6 ▪ Evaluating an image

If your critical reading moves on to evaluation, you'll form judgments about the quality and significance of the image: Is the message of the image accurate and fair, or is it distorted and biased? Can you support, refute, or extend the message? Does the image achieve its apparent purpose, and is the purpose worthwhile? How does the image affect you?

You can read Matthew Greene's response to the *BoostUp.org* advertisement by following the links in the e-book version of this handbook at *mycomplab.com*.

Exercise 5 **Viewing an image critically**

Review the list of visual elements earlier in this chapter and then take another close look at the *BoostUp.org* advertisement or the photograph opposite. Using the guidelines on the preceding pages, draw your own conclusions about one of the images. Write while reading and thinking to help yourself concentrate and develop ideas.

The North American

Richard Rodriquez

It is instinctive in humans, as it is in other warm-blooded creatures, to fear the swallower. I had an uncle who came from India and who feared being deported by U.S. immigration officials because he feared India would swallow him - consume, devour him again - without respect for his person or his life's journey, a journey that brought him to Sacramento, California, where he wished to remain. An American. Americans have lately taken up a Canadian word -multiculturalism - as a talisman against the notion of the swallower. But America has always been the swallower. Our national culture has been omnivorous. I believe the United States of America swallowed me a long time ago. It may be that I am about to swallow you.

There is something unsettling about immigrants because they can seem to overturn America—or they can seem to undo America. At the very point at which Americans think we have a communal identity, at the very point at which we think we know who we are—we are Protestants, culled from Western Europe, are we not?—then new immigrants appear from Southern Europe or from Eastern Europe. Suddenly we don't know exactly what the latest comers mean to our community or our identity, how they fit. Thus are we led to question our identity. After a generation or two, the grandchildren or the great-grandchildren of immigrants to the United States will romanticize the immigrant, will see the immigrant as precisely the meaning of America, to see the immigrant— who comes and remakes herself in this new land—as the figure who teaches us most about what it means to be an American. The immigrant, in mythic terms, travels from the outermost rind of America to the very center of the country's mythology. None of this, of course, do we say to the Vietnamese immigrant who serves us our breakfast at the hotel. In another forty years, we will be prepared to say of the Vietnamese immigrant, that he, with his breakfast tray, with his intuition for travel, he alone realizes the meaning of America.

In 1997 the Gallup Poll conducted a survey on race relations in America. The pollster found that race relations in America strained as respondents ascended an economic ladder. For example, college-educated blacks were pessimistic about interracial relationships. But the poll was only concerned with white and black Americans. No question was asked of the Vietnamese man who served me breakfast today in the hotel. There was certainly no reference to the Chinese grocer at the corner. There was no reference to the Guatemalans in San Francisco or to the Salvadorans who re-roofed my Victorian house. None at all. That is because the American conversation about race has always been an abstract in white and black. What I represent, in my public life, is a kind of rude intrusion into the black-and-white conversation. Though I was born in San Francisco, I assume the outsider's task of unsettling the United States of America. I have listened to the black-and-white conversation for most of my life and it had nothing to do with me. I was supposed to attach myself to one side or the other, without asking the obvious questions: What is this white-and-black dialectic? Why does it admit so little reference to anyone else?

Brown does not represent a third race, but rather some blurring of racial distinction. I am speaking to you in American English that was taught me by Irish nuns, immigrant women, in California. I wear an Indian face; I answer to a Spanish surname as well as this California first name, Richard. You might wonder about the complexity of historical factors, the collision of centuries, that creates Richard Rodriguez. My brownness is the illustration of that collision, or the bland memorial of it. I stand before you as an impure-American. An ambiguous-American. I address you from the pride of my impurity. In the nineteenth century, Texans used to say that the reason that Mexicans were so easily defeated in battle was because we were so dilute, being neither pure Indian nor pure Spaniard. In the nineteenth century, Mexicans used to say that Mexico, the country of my ancestry, joined two worlds. José Vasconcelos, the Mexican educator and philosopher, famously described Mexicans as *la raza cosmica*, the cosmic race. In Mexico what one finds as early as the eighteenth century is a predominant population of mixed-race people. The *mestizo* predominated over the pure European and the pure Indian. Also, once the slave had been freed in Mexico, the intermarriage rate between the Indian and the African in Mexico was greater than in any other country in the Americas and has not been equaled since.

Race mixture has not been a point of pride in the United States. Americans speak more easily about diversity than we do about the fact that I might marry your daughter; you might become we; we might eat the same food. We settle more easily on the Canadian notion of diversity because it preserves the notion that we are separate, that our elbows do not have to touch, much less merge; that I need not become you, that I can remain Mexican, whatever that mean, in the United States of America. I would argue that instead of adopting the Canadian model of multiculturalism, the United States might begin to imagine the Mexican alternative of a *mestizaje* society, and move away from the multicultural safety that Canada offers, and all fear of swallowing, of being swallowed.

I was born in Mexico, therefore—though I wasn't. I was born in San Francisco to Mexican immigrant parents. But I was reinvented in 1973 by Richard Nixon. Nixon had instructed the Office of Management and Budget to determine the major racial and ethnic groups in this country. (Can you imagine the bureaucratic deliberation over the phone books of America?) The Office of Management and Budget came up with five major ethnic or racial groups. The groups are, in no order of preference, white, black, Asian/Pacific Islander, American Indian, and Hispanic.

I call myself Hispanic.

The interesting thing about Hispanics is that you will never meet us in Latin America. You may meet Chileans and Peruvians and Mexicans. You will not meet Hispanics. If you inquire in Lima or Bogota about Hispanics, you will be referred to Dallas. For "Hispanic" is a gringo contrivance, a definition of the world that suggests that I have more in common with Argentine Italians than I have with American Indians; that there is an ineffable union between the white Cuban and the mulatto Puerto Rican. Nixon's conclusion has become the basis for the way we now organize and understand our society. As a Hispanic, I will say with some irony that a recent statistic from the Census Bureau interests me very much. The Census Bureau tells us that by the year 2003 Hispanics will outnumber blacks to become the largest minority in the United States. While I admit a competition exists in America between Hispanic and black, I insist that the comparison of Hispanics to blacks will lead, ultimately, to complete nonsense. For there is no such thing as a Hispanic race. There is no Hispanic race in the world. In Latin America, you see every race of the world. You see white Hispanics, you see black Hispanics, you see brown Hispanics who are Indians, many of whom do not speak Spanish because they resisted. You see Asian Hispanics. To compare blacks and Hispanics, therefore, is to construct a fallacious equation.

Some Hispanics have accepted the fiction. Some Hispanics have too easily accustomed themselves to impersonating a third race, a great new third race in America. But Hispanic is an ethnic term. It is a term denoting culture. So when the Census Bureau says by the year 2060 one-third of all Americans will identify themselves as Hispanic, the Census Bureau is not speculating in pigmen,. but rather is predicting how by the year 2060 one-third of all Americans will identify themselves culturally. The black Dominican today who identifies himself as Hispanic is identifying himself in terms of culture rather than by race, and that is revolutionary.
For a country that traditionally has taken its understandings of community from blood and color, to have so large a group of Americans identify themselves by virtue of language or fashion or cuisine or literature is an extraordinary change, and a revolutionary one.

Is there, in fact, a Hispanic culture? Henry Cisneros, the ex-mayor of San Antonio, gathered together a group of Hispanic politicians in the mid-1990s to try to determine whether there was a Hispanic political agenda, for, indeed, there is a Hispanic caucus in Washington modeled on the African American caucus in Washington. After two weeks the group that Henry Cisneros convened could not come up with an agenda. There is no Hispanic politics. What unites the eighth-generation New Mexican, who considers himself a Spaniard, with the white Republican Cuban with the black Puerto-Rican with the Guatemalan Indian who arrived in San Diego yesterday with the Mexican American gang kids who speak Spanglish in East L.A.? What singular culture is there in this diverse company?

Some Hispanics speak Spanish. Some do not. Some are Catholic. Many are becoming Evangelical Protestants. Some are white. Some are brown. Some are black. The more I think about it, the more I think there are only two considerations common to Hispanics. First, this business of impurity, that we are making America an impure place. The second thing that unites Hispanics is that we (those of us who are not of Europe) look south when we consider the past. That is our revolutionary gift to America, the cultural inheritance that we bring to this country. Hispanics are changing the contour of the United States because we are north-south people. The United States has traditionally written its history east to west, has begun its history at Plymouth Rock and has ended up at Venice Beach, a country that has always understood itself in one direction only. Suddenly, there are millions of Americans who see themselves along a north-south trajectory. That is a revolutionary regard.

After the North American Free Trade Agreement (NAFTA) was signed by the presidents of Mexico and the United States and the prime minister of Canada, the New York Times called me to ask if I would write something on NAFTA. I said I couldn't write anything on NAFTA, because I've never met a North American. But then I thought, actually, I do know one North American. He is a Mexican from the state of Oaxaca in southern Mexico. He impersonates an Italian chef in a restaurant in the Napa Valley for about nine months of the year. He is trilingual. He is a Mixteco Indian. His first language belongs to that tribe. His second language is Spanish, the language of his Colonial oppressors. His third language is a working knowledge of English, because, after all, he works here. He deals with two currencies, two codes of justice, two views of the human condition.

The North American knows thousands of miles of dirt roads and freeways. He knows where to hide in the United States, because he is, after all, illegal when he crosses the dangerous border. On the Mexican side, he knows how to hide from the Mexican federal police who are always trying to steal his money. He wires his money home by Western Union, he puts the rest in his shoes. In Mexico, he lives in a sixteenth-century village where the Virgen de Guadalupe floats over his wife's bed. In Napa Valley, too, he hears Madonna, "the material girl." He is the first North American. He sees this hemisphere whole. He is a peasant from Latin America. At the Harvard Business School, meanwhile, there is much talk about this new North American, this transborder reality. Harvard conceives the pan-American as a new idea, patented by MBAs, but the peasant has known the idea all his life.

There is a quarrel going on in California about mythology: Which myth applies? What does California mean? What is California? For a long time the United States labored under the impression that California was the Far West. "Go west. young man." Go west, young man, and change the color of your hair and go to Gold's Gym, get a new body, lose weight, become a movie star, Botox your name, become Rock Hudson. But, as early as the 1860s, California was finitude. We had come to the end of the road in California to discover that America was a finite idea. I think the innovation in California results from that idea of finitude— land's end. Americans have been trained by their maps to believe that everything will be OK if we move west. But having arrived at the end, what do we do? We look to the sky. It is no coincidence that so much technological innovation is happening along the strip of land that stretches from North County, San Diego, all the way to Redmond, Washington. Why there? Why are people entering cyberspace with such frenzy at the western portal? Because restlessness continues and because the land has come to an end. But has it? Today—in about an hour from now—a procession of planes will land at LAX from Asia. The flights originate in Asia. We are sort of glad to see Asians. but we don't have any more room in California. We've come to the end of things in California. But the Asian says, "Well, you know, I've always thought this was where America begins. I thought this was where the continent begins." What would the history of America look like if it were written in reverse, from west to east? Have we even imagined such a history?

People in Mexico go to el Norte not because they want to find a new future; they go to el Norte because they want a dreary job working at a dry cleaner's in L.A. They work to sustain the past. People climb to el Norte without experiencing the same sense of disconnection from the past that the Western traveler felt. If one travels east to west, one follows the light of day; one leaves the past behind. If one travels north and south, one begins to resemble a monarch butterfly or a whale. One moves with seasons. Laborers who worked six months of the year in the North and returned south every year infuriated Americans, because Americans didn't understand what that north-south journey might mean. Americans could only imagine disruption. Discontinuity. A new day. But now Americans are becoming north-south people. There are grandmothers in Minnesota who live not by some east-west calendar, but by a north-south calendar. They spend summer in Minneapolis and winter in Florida. All over the country I meet teenagers who are not traveling between coasts, as we used to imagine youth's journey in America, but between hot and cold, between desert and tundra—the new extremities of the country, the new way the country exists in the American imagination.

To my mind, nothing else Bill Clinton accomplished compares to NAFTA. The notion given to the United States by this trade agreement is that the United States is related to Canada, is related to Mexico. Northern Mexico looks like San Diego these days. Northern Mexico is filled with Gold's Gyms and Hard Rock Cafes, shopping centers. Everybody wants to be an American in northern Mexico. And South Texas is becoming very Mexican. That circumstance surprises Americans because our notion of community never extended beyond our borders and certainly never extended south. Look at the map now—the Hispanic map of the United States of America—and one of the weirdest things you will notice is the reconquest of the Spanish Empire. Florida, Colorado, New Mexico, Arizona, Texas, California, and Nevada are Hispanic—just as they were in the early eighteenth century.

I know there are concerns about diminished civility and social fragmentation in the United States, and especially in a city like Los Angeles. But there are uses of incivility, too. The formation ofa society does not happen easily. It does not happen when all of us feel good about each other, and it does not happen because we all like each other. Coca-Cola commissioned a commercial to run at Christmas time wherein a utopian population, in various ethnic costumes, in mutual respect and good will, sing a hymn to Coca-Cola. All of us in America have been encouraged thus to believe in a relative and banal multiculturalism. But the real working out of inevitability more often happens at some Frontage Road franchise where the red-headed waitress has to communicate with the Mexican fry-cook, and she doesn't have all the right words. and neither does he. And so their cooperation—entirely pragmatic—ends up sounding like this: "Dos huevos, over easy, side of salchiche!"

In 1992, Los Angeles endured one of the great urban riots of American history, a terrible event that began as a black-and-white altercation, but within hours drew Korean shopkeepers, then Salvadoran women who wrestled with Mexican women outside Kmart for looted boxes of Pampers. You cannot have a black-and-white riot in a multiracial city. The most interesting thing about that riot was the way the city got formed from the terror of those days and nights. On the West Side of the city, that first Thursday, one saw neighborhoods on television that one had never visited. L.A. was famous, after all, as the city of separate suburbs, and separate freeway exits. The interesting thing was the way those distant neighborhoods drew closer and closer and closer together. By about four A.M., people on the West Side began to hear fire sirens, began to smell smoke. For the first time, Los Angeles realized it was one city. This realization did not come from good feeling. It came from terror. People resorted to their closets for guns. People came to realize the street they live on is, in fact, connected to every other street.

Sometimes I stand on the line between San Diego and Tijuana, and I talk to the kids who are beginning their American lives. I do not talk to them about Benjamin Franklin or Tom Paine. They've never heard of the Bill of Rights. They are coming, they say—many of them illegally—because there is a job in Glendale waiting for them or there is a grower near Tracy who needs them to pick peaches. That's it. They are not coming for welfare. They are not coming for famous freedoms. There is no politician who will tell the truth about these young men and women. The truth is that we cannot stop them from coming. The fact is there is a 2,000-mile border that cannot be defended. Americans continue to worry about illegal immigration. But the poor cannot be stopped. The poor, worldwide, are mobile. We of the middle class do not know how to stop them, how to keep them out of our society, and the truth is that we don't want to keep them out of our society. These Mexican kids know that. They know we will hire them to sit patiently with our dying mother. They know we will hire them to spade the moats around our rose bushes. They know we will hire them. In Mexico, in the realm of the public, the politician will say one thing and everyone will assume the opposite to be true. The Mexican judge says, "five years"; the family of the defendant calculates one year or despair. The price of the jar of baby food says 50 pesos and it might be 50 pesos or it might be 10. Nothing is what it seems in the public realm. Mexicans transfer this knowledge to America. They know that public utterance of prohibition means one thing and private welcome means another. There is work in San Diego if you can make it across.

In the 1970s, people began to believe that L.A. might not be a West Coast city with palm trees and beachfront, but might, in fact, be a northern desert city with Indians, sand, sirocco. The moment the mythology of that city began to change from blond to brown—Los Angelinos began to make the best of inevitability. They began to bring cactus into the house. They took the curtains off the windows and extolled the beauty of desert light. By adopting a desert aesthetic, Los Angeles attempted to transform something fearful; to make beautiful something that was fearful. Fear is not always met with withdrawal; sometimes fear is met by a kind of seduction. One solution to the fear of the advent of a brown population is to cast the brown man or woman in a soap opera; to call him the newest, sexiest; to fall in love with her. We lock up black males at a disproportionate rate because we are afraid of black males and we don't know what to do with black males—that's why we dance to black music. We end up marrying Chinese women. We also don't know what to do with empowered Western women who are more like black males than they are like Chinese women. In the great ancient societies, France would marry England—the king would pawn his daughter to England—as a way of making England part of the family. We are giving each other our daughters. We are marrying each other as much out of fear as of yearning.

People ask me all the time, "Do you envision another Quebec forming in this country from all of this immigrant movement? Do you see a Quebec forming in the

Southwest, for example?" No, I don't see that at all. I do see something different happening with the immigrant population, which is as much as ten years younger than the U.S. national population, and which is more fertile than the U.S. national population. I see the movement of the immigrant as the movement of youth into a country that is growing middle-aged. Immigrants are the archetypal Americans at a time when we—U.S. citizens—have become post-Americans.

Once more along the border: I met three boys from a group called Victory Outreach, an evangelical Protestant group that works with young people who have serious drug or gang problems. Here they were (five hundred years after Columbus), here were these three Indians who told me that they were coming to the United States of America to convert the United States of America to Protestantism. This doesn't sound like Quebec. This sounded like immigrants are bringing America to America—a gift.

I was at a small Apostolic Assembly in East Palo Alto a few years ago, a mainly Spanish-speaking congregation, along the freeway, near the heart of the Silicon Valley. This is the other side. It used to be black East Palo Alto. It's quickly becoming Asian and Hispanic Palo Alto—the same story. There was a moment in the service when newcomers to the congregation were introduced to the entire group. They brought letters of introduction from sister churches in Latin America. The minister read the various letters and announced the names and places of origin to the community. Everyone applauded. And I thought to myself: It's over. The border is over. These people were not being asked whether they had a green card. They were not being asked whether they're legally here or illegally here. They were being welcomed within this community for reasons of culture. There is now a north-south line that is theological, and it cannot be circumvented by the U.S. Border Patrol.

The deepest fear Americans conceive of the South right now is not of the separateness of the South, but that people of the South will replace us, that they want us, that they want to be us, that they want our food, that they want our culture, that we will be swallowed. One Monday, a few years ago, Monday Night Football originated from Monterrey, Mexico—a northern Mexican metropolis with all the charm of Pittsburgh in the 1930s. The pre-game show began with a serenade by a group of *mariachis*, singing in Spanish. What the *mariachis* sang was this: The Dallas Cowboys are our team. They are Mexico's team. And I thought,does anybody at ABC News know about this? Do any of us realize that the Dallas Cowboys are about to be devoured?

Americans continue to believe that Canadian multiculturalism is going to make everything come out all right. Multiculturalism is not going to make everything come out all right. You—here I address America—you are going to end up with Mexican grandchildren.

I was on a BBC interview show, and a woman introduced me as being "in favor" of assimilation. I am not in favor of assimilation any more than I am in favor of the Pacific Ocean. If I had a bumper sticker, it would read something like ASSIMILATION HAPPENS. One doesn't get up in the morning, as an immigrant child in America, and think to oneself, "How much of an American will I become today?" One doesn't walk down the street and decide to be 40 percent Mexican and 60 percent American. Culture is fluid. Culture is smoke in the air. You breathe it. You eat it. You notice culture or you don't. Elvis Presley goes in your ear and you cannot get Elvis Presley out of your mind. He's in there. I'm in favor of assimilation. I'm not in favor of assimilation. I recognize that it exists. L.A. has become Mexican, which is what it always was. L.A., this monstrous city that we identify now as the immigrant capital of America, has three times the miscegenation rate of the American average. I was in Merced, California, a few years ago, which is a town of about 75,000 people in the Central Valley of Califomia. Merced's two largest immigrant groups now are Laotian Hmong and Mexicans. The Laotians have never in the history of the world, as far as I know, lived next to the Mexicans. But there they are in Merced, and they are living next to the Mexicans. They don't like each other. I was talking to the Laotian kids about why they don't like the Mexican kids. They were telling me this and that—the Mexicans do this and the Mexicans don't do that—when I suddenly realized these Laotian kids were speaking English with a Spanish accent.

I remember when once Bill Moyers asked me how I thought of myself, as an American or Hispanic. I said, "I'm Chinese." And that's because I live in a Chinese city and that's because I want to be Chinese. Well, why not?

Yes, I think it's a celebration of utopianism. I do think distinctions exist. I'm not talking about an America tomorrow in which we're going to find black and white no longer the distinguishing marks of separateness. But for many, many young people that I meet, it sounds almost Victorian to talk about their identity that way. They don't think of themselves in those terms. And they're already moving into a world in which skin or tattoo or ornament or movement or commune or sexuality or drug are the organizing principles of their identity. And the notion that they are white or black simply doesn't apply to them. And increasingly, of course, you meet children who really don't know how to say what they are anymore. They simply are too many things. We're in such a world, in such an America, already. What will we say—that we still live in a black and white America? I mean, what do we say to Tiger Woods, who insisted he's not African, because that would deny his mother's existence? I met a young girl in San Diego the other day at a convention of mixed race children, among whom the common habit is to define one parent over the other. In most white and black marriages, the habit is to define black over white. But this girl said that her mother was Mexican and her father was African. I said, "What are you?" She said, "Black-xican." And I think to myself, "You know, the vocabulary that the Spanish empire has, the recognition of multiplicity of possibilities, we do not have in this society—we do not have words to describe who we are anymore. And I tell you, if we rely on the old vocabulary, we are doomed because no one is using it anymore. They're inventing their own words."

So, what myth do we tell ourselves? You know, I think the person who got closest to it was Karl Marx. Marx predicted that the discovery of gold in California would be a more central event to the Americas than the discovery of the Americas by Columbus. He goes on to write that the discovery of the Americas by Columbus was only the meeting of two tribes, essentially, the European and the Indian. But he said, "You know, when gold was discovered in California in the 1840s, the entire world met." For the first time in human history, all of the known world gathered. The Malaysian was in the gold fields alongside the African, alongside the Chinese, alongside the Australian, alongside the American pioneer, etc., etc., etc.

For the first time—and with calamitous results—the whole world was seeking gold in the same place at the same time, and they were at each other's throats. People were murdered and so forth. But that was an event without parallel, and it is, I think. the beginning of modern California and why California, today, really is our mythology. It provides the mythological structure for understanding how we might talk about the American experience as not being biracial, but the experience of the recreation of the known world in the New World.

Sometimes the truly revolutionary things that are going on in this society are happening almost regardless and almost without anybody being aware of them. We are going to wake up one day, and it's all going to be changed, and we're going to say, "When did it all change? Why didn't the *New York Times* tell us it was going to happen? Where was Maureen Dowd when we needed her?" She was going on about Bill Clinton's sex life.

There is no black race. There is no white race either. There are mythologies, and I'm in the business—insofar as I'm in any business at all—of demythologizing these identities, and suggesting their complexity and the dynamism of individuals to meet and learn and fall in love with people different from themselves.

So I come to you as a man of many cultures. I come to you as a Chinese, and unless you understand that I am Chinese, then you've not understood anything I've said.

Unit 3

Unit 3 Interweavings

Richard Rodriguez writes, "Culture is fluid. Culture is the smoke in the air." Having just explored the idea of the border from the stance of immigration and acculturation, we will now delve further into the concept of U.S. culture(s), recognizing that culture flows across borders (national, societal, individual) in ways we may not have considered before. We will also investigate the overlapping areas between and among cultures and the way identities are constructed in these multilayered spaces.

The Writing Situation

The Writing Situation

How should I tackle a writing assignment?

Many writers find it helpful to break writing tasks into manageable steps. Such steps are part of the **writing process**—the term for all the activities, mental and physical, that go into creating what eventually becomes a finished piece of work.

There is no one writing process: no two writers proceed in the same way, and even an individual writer adapts his or her process to the task at hand. Still, most experienced writers pass through certain stages that overlap and circle back on one another:

- **Analyzing the writing situation,** especially considering subject, audience, and purpose.
- **Invention and planning:** generating ideas, gathering information, focusing on a central theme, and organizing material.
- **Drafting:** expressing and connecting ideas.
- **Revising and editing:** rethinking and improving structure, content, style, and presentation.

As you complete varied assignments and try the many techniques included in this book, you will develop your own writing process.

a Analyze the writing situation.

Any writing you do for others occurs in a **writing situation** that both limits and clarifies your choices. You are communicating within a particular context, about a particular subject, to a particular audience of readers, for a specific reason. You may need to conduct research. You probably face a length requirement and a deadline. And you may be expected to present your work in a certain format.

Analyzing the elements of the writing situation at the very start of a project can tell you much about how to proceed. (For discussion of the following elements, refer to the page numbers given.)

Context

- **What is your writing for?** A course in school? Work? Something else? What are the requirements for writing in this context?
- **Will you present your writing on paper, online, or orally?** What does the presentation method require in preparation time, special skills, and use of technology?

mycomplab

Visit *mycomplab.com* for more resources and exercises on the writing situation.

- **How much leeway do you have for this writing?** What does the stated or implied assignment tell you?

Subject

- **What does your writing assignment instruct you to write about?** If you don't have a specific assignment, what do you want to write about?
- **What interests you about the subject?** What do you already have ideas about or want to know more about?
- **What does the assignment require you to do with the subject?**

Purpose

- **What aim does your assignment specify?** For instance, does it ask you to explain something or argue a point?
- **Why are you writing?** What do you want your work to accomplish? What effect do you intend it to have on readers?
- **How can you best achieve your purpose?**

Audience

- **Who will read your writing?**
- **What do your readers already know and think about your subject?** Do they have any characteristics—such as educational background, experience in your field, or political views—that could influence their reception of your writing?
- **How should you project yourself in your writing?** What role should you play in relation to readers, and what information should you give? How informal or formal should your writing be?
- **What do you want readers to do or think after they read your writing?**

Research

- **What kinds of evidence will best suit your subject, purpose, and audience?** What combination of facts, examples, and expert opinions will support your ideas?
- **Does your assignment require research?** Will you need to consult sources of information or conduct other research, such as interviews, surveys, or experiments?
- **Even if research is not required, what additional information do you need to develop your subject?** How will you obtain it?
- **What style should you use to cite your sources?**

Deadline and length

- **When is the assignment due?** How will you complete the work you have to do in the available time?
- **How long should your writing be?** If no length is assigned, what seems appropriate for your subject, purpose, and audience?

Document design

- **What organization and format does the assignment require?**
- **How might you use margins, headings, and other elements to achieve your purpose?**
- **How might you use graphs, photographs, or other illustrations to support ideas and interest readers?**

Exercise 1 Analyzing a writing situation

The following assignment was made in a survey course in psychology. What does the assignment specify and imply about the elements of the writing situation? Given this assignment, how would you answer the questions on the preceding pages and above?

When is psychotherapy most likely to work? That is, what combinations of client, therapist, and theory tend to achieve good results? In your discussion, cite studies supporting your conclusions. Length: 1500 to 1800 words. Post your paper online to me and your discussion group by March 30.

b Find an appropriate subject.

A subject for writing has several basic requirements:

- **It should be suitable for the assignment.**
- **It should be neither too general nor too limited for the assigned deadline and paper length.**
- **It should be something you are willing to learn more about, even something you care about.**

When you receive an assignment, study its wording and its implications about your writing situation to guide your choice of subject:

- **What's wanted from you?** Many writing assignments contain words such as *discuss, describe, analyze, report, interpret, explain, define, argue,* or *evaluate*. These words specify the way you are to approach your subject, what kind of thinking is expected of you, and what your general purpose is.
- **For whom are you writing?** Many assignments will specify your readers, but sometimes you will have to figure out for yourself who your audience is and what it expects of you.
- **What kind of research is required?** An assignment may specify the kinds of sources you are expected to consult, and you can use such information to choose your subject. (If you are unsure whether research is required, check with your instructor.)

- **Does the subject need to be narrowed?** To do the subject justice in the length and time required, you'll often need to limit it. (See below.)

Answering these questions about your assignment will help set some boundaries for your choice of subject. Then you can explore your own interests and experiences to narrow the subject so that you can cover it adequately within the space and time assigned. Federal aid to college students could be the subject of a book; the kinds of aid available or why the government should increase aid would be a more appropriate subject for a four-page paper due in a week.

One helpful technique for narrowing a subject is to ask focused questions about it, seeking one that seems appropriate for your assignment and that promises to sustain your interest through the writing process. The following examples illustrate how questioning can scale down broad subjects to specific subjects that are limited and manageable:

Broad subjects	Specific subjects
Social-networking sites	What draws people to these sites? How do the sites alter the ways people interact? What privacy protections should the sites provide for users?
Mrs. Mallard in Kate Chopin's "The Story of an Hour"	What changes does Mrs. Mallard undergo? Why does Mrs. Mallard respond as she does to news of her husband's death? What does the story's irony contribute to the character of Mrs. Mallard?
Lincoln's weaknesses as President	What was Lincoln's most significant error as commander-in-chief of the Union army? Why did Lincoln delay emancipating the slaves? Why did Lincoln have difficulties controlling his cabinet?

Use the following guidelines to narrow broad subjects:

- **Ask as many questions about your broad subject as you can think of.** Make a list.
- **For each question that interests you and fits the assignment, roughly sketch out the main ideas.** Consider how many paragraphs or pages of specific facts, examples, and other details you would need to pin those ideas down. This thinking should give you at least a vague idea of how much work you'd have to do and how long the resulting paper might be.
- **Break a too-broad question down further,** repeating the previous steps.

The Internet can also help you limit a general subject. Browsing a directory such as *BUBL LINK* (*bubl.ac.uk/link*), pursue increasingly narrow categories to find a suitably limited topic.

Exercise 2 Narrowing subjects

Choose three of the following broad subjects and, using the techniques above, narrow each one to at least one specific question that can be answered in a three- to four-page paper.

1. Use of cell phones
2. Training of teachers
3. Dance in America
4. The history of women's suffrage
5. Food additives
6. Immigrants in the United States
7. Space exploration
8. African Americans and civil rights
9. Child abuse
10. Successes in cancer research
11. Television evangelism
12. Women writers
13. Campaign finance reform
14. Genetic engineering
15. Trends in popular music

c Define your purpose.

Your **purpose** in writing is your chief reason for communicating something about your subject to a particular audience of readers. Most writing you do will have one of four main purposes:

- **To entertain readers.**
- **To express your feelings or ideas.**
- **To explain something to readers (exposition).**
- **To persuade readers to accept or act on your opinion (argument).**

These purposes often overlap in a single essay, but usually one predominates. And the dominant purpose will influence your slant on your subject, the details you choose, and even the words you use.

Many writing assignments narrow the purpose by using a signal word, such as the following:

- **Report:** survey, organize, and objectively present the available evidence on the subject.
- **Summarize:** concisely state the main points in a text, argument, theory, or other work.
- **Discuss:** examine the main points, competing views, or implications of the subject.
- **Compare and contrast:** explain the similarities and differences between two subjects.
- **Define:** specify the meaning of a term or a concept—distinctive characteristics, boundaries, and so on.
- **Analyze:** identify the elements of the subject and discuss how they work together.

- **Interpret:** infer the subject's meaning or implications.
- **Evaluate:** judge the quality or significance of the subject, considering pros and cons.
- **Argue:** take a position on the subject and support your position with evidence.

You can conceive of your purpose more specifically, too, in a way that incorporates your particular subject and the outcome you intend:

To explain how Annie Dillard's "Total Eclipse" builds to its climax so that readers appreciate the author's skill.

To explain the steps in a new office procedure so that staffers will be able to follow it without difficulty.

To persuade readers to support the college administration's plan for more required courses.

To argue against additional regulation of handguns so that readers will perceive the potential disadvantages for themselves and for the nation as a whole.

d Consider your audience.

The readers likely to see your work—your **audience**—will often be specified or implied in a writing assignment. When you write an editorial for the student newspaper, your audience consists of fellow students. When you analyze a poem in a literature class, your audience consists of your instructor and perhaps your classmates. The box on the next page gives questions that can help you define the audience in most writing situations.

Your sense of your audience will influence three key elements of what you write:

- **The specific information you use to gain and keep the attention of readers and guide them to accept your conclusions.** This information may consist of details, facts, examples, and other evidence that make your ideas clear, support your assertions, and suit your readers' needs.
- **The role you choose to play in relation to your readers.** Depending on your purpose, you will want readers to perceive you in a certain way. The possible roles are many and varied—for instance, scholar, storyteller, lecturer, guide, reporter, advocate, inspirer.
- **The tone you use. Tone** in writing is the attitude conveyed by words and sentence structures. Depending on your aims and what you think your readers will expect and respond to, your tone may be formal or informal. The attitude you convey may be serious or light, forceful or calm, irritated or cheerful.

Questions about audience

Identity and expectations

- **Who *are* my readers?**
- **What do my readers expect from the kind of writing I'm doing?** Do they expect features such as a particular organization and format, distinctive kinds of evidence, or a certain style of documenting sources?
- **What do I want readers to know or do after reading my work?** How should I make that clear to them?
- **How should I project myself to my readers?** How formal or informal will they expect me to be? What role and tone should I assume?

Characteristics, knowledge, and attitudes

- **What characteristics of readers are relevant for my subject and purpose?** For instance:

  Age and sex
  Occupation: students, professional colleagues, etc.
  Social or economic role: car buyers, potential employers, etc.
  Economic or educational background
  Ethnic background
  Political, religious, or moral beliefs and values
  Hobbies or activities

- **How will the characteristics of readers influence their attitudes toward my subject?**
- **What do readers already know and *not* know about my topic?** How much do I have to tell them?
- **How should I handle any specialized terms?** Will readers know them? If not, should I define them?
- **What ideas, arguments, or information might surprise, excite, or offend readers?** How should I handle these points?
- **What misconceptions might readers have of my subject and/or my approach to it?** How can I dispel these misconceptions?

Uses and format

- **What will readers do with my writing?** Should I expect them to read every word from the top, to scan for information, or to look for conclusions? Can I help with a summary, headings, illustrations, or other aids?

Your information, role, and tone contribute to your writer's **voice:** your projection of yourself into your writing. Your voice conveys your sense of the world as it applies to the particular writing situation: this subject, this purpose, this audience. Thus voice can vary quite a bit from one writing situation to another, as the following memos illustrate. Both have the same subject and general purpose, but they address different readers.

To coworkers

Ever notice how much paper collects in your trash basket every day? Well, most of it can be recycled with little effort, I promise. Basically, all you need to do is set a bag or box near your desk and deposit wastepaper in it. I know, space is cramped in these little cubicles. But what's a little more crowding when the earth's at stake? . . .

Voice: a peer who is thoughtful, cheerful, and sympathetic

Information: how employees could handle recycling; no mention of costs

Role: colleague

Tone: informal, personal (*Ever notice; Well; you; I know, space is cramped*)

To management

In my four months here, I have observed that all of us throw out baskets of potentially recyclable paper every day. Considering the drain on our forest resources and the pressure on landfills that paper causes, we could make a valuable contribution to the environmental movement by helping to recycle the paper we use. At the company where I worked before, the employees separate clean wastepaper from other trash at their desks. The maintenance staff collects trash in two receptacles, and the trash hauler (the same one we use here) makes separate pickups. I do not know what the hauler charges for handling recyclable material. . . .

Voice: a subordinate who is thoughtful, responsible, and serious

Information: specific reasons; view of company as a whole; reference to another company; problem of cost

Role: employee

Tone: formal, serious (*Considering the drain; forest resources; valuable contribution;* no *you*)

CULTURE LANGUAGE If English is not your native language, you may not be accustomed to appealing to your readers when you write. In some cultures, for instance, readers may accept a writer's statements with little or no questioning. When writing in English, try to reach out to readers by being accurate, fair, interesting, and clear.

If You Are What You Eat, Then What Am I?

Geeta Kothari

Geeta Kothari came with her parents from India as a child. She lived with them in the United States with her sister but far from her extended family in northern India. She married an American and became a writing instructor at the University of Pittsburgh. Her edited collection Did My Mama Like to Dance and Other Stories about Mothers and Daughters *(1994), as well as many stories and articles in magazines and newspapers, have earned her recognition as an important present-day writer. In this essay, she asks about the identity of people like her who have grown up between cultures. She uses her experiences with both American and Indian food to define the predicament of her life. As a child, she wanted to be like other children and eat sandwiches, but her mother had no idea how to make American sandwiches. At the same time, when she visited India with her parents, she could not tolerate the types of bacteria that populated Indian drink and food. She became ill by merely drinking from a bottle of Fanta soda. After marrying her husband, she found herself repelled by the smell of meat on his skin, never being able herself to face a rare steak or even a pork chop. This essay investigates the links in her life between food and identity. It is part of a longer work from the* Kenyon Review.

To belong is to understand the tacit codes of the people you live with.
—Michael Ignatieff, *Blood and Belonging*

Reprinted from *Kenyon Review* 21, no. 1 (winter 1999), by permission of the author and the Kenyon Review.

1 The first time my mother and I open a can of tuna, I am nine years old. We stand in the doorway of the kitchen, in semi-darkness, the can tilted toward daylight. I want to eat what the kids at school eat: bologna, hot dogs, salami—foods my parents find repugnant because they contain pork and meat byproducts, crushed bone and hair glued together by chemicals and fat. Although she has never been able to tolerate the smell of fish, my mother buys the tuna, hoping to satisfy my longing for American food. 1

Indians, of course, do not eat such things.

The tuna smells fishy, which surprises me because I can't remember anyone's tuna sandwich actually smelling like fish. And the tuna in those sandwiches doesn't look like this, pink and shiny, like an internal organ. In fact, this looks similar to the bad foods my mother doesn't want me to eat. She is silent, holding her face away from the can while peering into it like a half-blind bird.

"What's wrong with it?" I ask.

5 She has no idea. My mother does not know that the tuna everyone else's mothers made for them was tuna *salad*. 5

"Do you think it's botulism?"

I have never seen botulism, but I have read about it, just as I have read about but never eaten steak and kidney pie.

There is so much my parents don't know. They are not like other parents, and they disappoint me and my sister. They are supposed to help us negotiate the world outside, teach us the signs, the clues to proper behavior: what to eat and how to eat it.

We have expectations, and my parents fail to meet them, especially my mother, who works full-time. I don't understand what it means, to have a mother who works outside and inside the home; I notice only the ways in which she disappoints me. She doesn't show up for school plays. She doesn't make chocolate-frosted cupcakes for my class. At night, if I want her attention, I have to sit in the kitchen and talk to her while she cooks the evening meal, attentive to every third or fourth word I say.

10 We throw the tuna away. This time my mother is disappointed. I go to school with tuna eaters. I see their sandwiches, yet cannot explain the discrepancy between them and the stinking, oily fish in my mother's hand. We do not understand so many things, my mother and I. 10

When we visit our relatives in India, food prepared outside the house is carefully monitored. In the hot, sticky monsoon months in New

Delhi and Bombay, we cannot eat ice cream, salad, cold food, or any fruit that can't be peeled. Definitely no meat. People die from amoebic dysentery, unexplained fevers, strange boils on their bodies. We drink boiled water only, no ice. No sweets except for jalebi, thin fried twists of dough in dripping hot sugar syrup. If we're caught outside with nothing to drink, Fanta, Limca, Thums Up (after Coca-Cola is thrown out by Mrs. Gandhi[1]) will do. Hot tea sweetened with sugar, served with thick creamy buffalo milk, is preferable. It should be boiled, to kill the germs on the cup.

My mother talks about "back home" as a safe place, a silk cocoon frozen in time where we are sheltered by family and friends. Back home, my sister and I do not argue about food with my parents. Home is where they know all the rules. We trust them to guide us safely through the maze of city streets for which they have no map, and we trust them to feed and take care of us, the way parents should.

Finally, though, one of us will get sick, hungry for the food we see our cousins and friends eating, too thirsty to ask for a straw, too polite to insist on properly boiled water.

At my uncle's diner in New Delhi, someone hands me a plate of aloo tikki, fried potato patties filled with mashed channa dal and served with a sweet and a sour chutney. The channa, mixed with hot chilies and spices, burns my tongue and throat. I reach for my Fanta, discard the paper straw, and gulp the sweet orange soda down, huge drafts that sting rather than soothe.

15 When I throw up later that day (or is it the next morning, when a 15
stomachache wakes me from deep sleep?), I cry over the frustration of being singled out, not from the pain my mother assumes I'm feeling as she holds my hair back from my face. The taste of orange lingers in my mouth, and I remember my lips touching the cold glass of the Fanta bottle.

At that moment, more than anything, I want to be like my cousins.

In New York, at the first Indian restaurant in our neighborhood, my father orders with confidence, and my sister and I play with the silverware until the steaming plates of lamb biryani arrive.

What is Indian food? my friends ask, their noses crinkling up.

Later, this restaurant is run out of business by the new Indo-Pak-Bangladeshi combinations up and down the street, which serve similar food. They use plastic cutlery and Styrofoam cups. They do not distinguish between North and South Indian cooking, or between Indian, Pakistani, and Bangladeshi cooking, and their customers do not care. The food is fast, cheap, and tasty. Dosa, a rice flour crepe stuffed with masala potato, appears on the same trays as chicken makhani.

20 Now my friends want to know, Do you eat curry at home? 20

One time my mother makes lamb vindaloo for guests. Like dosa, this is a South Indian dish, one that my Punjabi[2] mother has to learn from a cookbook. For us, she cooks everyday food—yellow dal, rice, chapati, bhaji. Lentils, rice, bread, and vegetables. She has never referred to anything on our table as "curry" or "curried," but I know she has made chicken curry for guests. Vindaloo, she explains, is a curry too. I understand then that curry is a dish created for guests, outsiders, a food for people who eat in restaurants.

I look around my boyfriend's freezer one day and find meat: pork chops, ground beef, chicken pieces, Italian sausage. Ham in the refrigerator, next to the homemade bolognese sauce. Tupperware filled with chili made from ground beef and pork.

He smells different from me. Foreign. Strange.

I marry him anyway.

25 He has inherited blue eyes that turn gray in bad weather, light brown hair, a sharp pointy nose, and excellent teeth. He learns to make chili with ground turkey and tofu, tomato sauce with red wine and portobello mushrooms, roast chicken with rosemary and slivers of garlic under the skin. 25

He eats steak when we are in separate cities, roast beef at his mother's house, hamburgers at work. Sometimes I smell them on his skin. I hope he doesn't notice me turning my face, a cheek instead of my lips, my nose wrinkled at the unfamiliar, musky smell.

I have inherited brown eyes, black hair, a long nose with a crooked bridge, and soft teeth with thin enamel. I am in my twenties, moving to a city far from my parents, before it occurs to me that jeera, the spice my sister avoids, must have an English name. I have to learn that haldi = turmeric, methi = fenugreek. What to make with fenugreek, I do not know. My grandmother used to make methi roti for our breakfast, cornbread with fresh fenugreek leaves served with a lump of homemade butter. No one makes it now that she's gone, though once in a while my mother will get a craving for it and produce a facsimile ("The cornmeal here is wrong") that only highlights what she's really missing: the smells and tastes of her mother's house.

I will never make my grandmother's methi roti or even my mother's unsatisfactory imitation of it. I attempt chapati; it takes six hours, three phone calls home, and leaves me with an aching back. I have to write translations down: jeera = cumin. My memory is unreliable. But I have always known garam = hot.

If I really want to make myself sick, I worry that my husband will one day leave me for a meat-eater, for someone familiar who doesn't sniff him suspiciously for signs of alimentary infidelity.

30 Indians eat lentils. I understand this as absolute, a decree from an 30 unidentifiable authority that watches and judges me.

So what does it mean that I cannot replicate my mother's dal? She and my father show me repeatedly, in their kitchen, in my kitchen. They coach me over the phone, buy me the best cookbooks, and finally write down their secrets. Things I'm supposed to know but don't. Recipes that should be, by now, engraved on my heart.

Living far from the comfort of people who require no explanation for what I do and who I am, I crave the foods we have shared. My mother convinces me that moong is the easiest dal to prepare, and yet it fails me every time: bland, watery, a sickly greenish yellow mush. These imperfact imitations remind me only of what I'm missing.

But I have never been fond of moong dal. At my mother's table it is the last thing I reach for. Now I worry that this antipathy toward dal signals something deeper, that somehow I am not my parents' daughter, not Indian, and because I cannot bear the touch and smell of raw meat, though I can eat it cooked (charred, dry, and overdone), I am not American either.

I worry about a lifetime purgatory in Indian restaurants where I will complain that all the food looks and tastes the same because they've used the same masala.

End Notes

1. Coca-Cola was banned in India for twenty years beginning in the mid-1970s, when Indira Gandhi was prime minister, because the company would not reveal its formula to the government. Fanta, Limca, and Thums Up are other soft drinks popular in India.
2. Native of the state of Punjab, in northern India.

The Changing Definition of African-American

Ira Berlin

One of the most prominent scholars of slavery and African-American history in the United States, Ira Berlin earned a Ph.D. from the University of Wisconsin in 1970. He has been a Fulbright professor at the University of Paris and has held fellowships at Princeton, Stanford, Harvard, and Australian National Universities. Berlin was a consultant to filmmaker Ken Burns's landmark Civil War *series on the PBS, and has worked closely with the Smithsonian Institution on Civil War and slavery programs. He has been a distinguished professor at Yale University and the University of Illinois, and is currently a distinguished professor at the University of Maryland. Berlin was founding editor of the Freedmen and Southern Society Project, which he directed until 1991. The project's multi-volume* Freedom: A Documentary History of Emancipation *(1982, 1985, 1990, 1993) won multiple awards from historical societies. Aided by funding from a number of prestigious foundations, including the National Endowment for the Humanities and the Ford Foundation, he has written several award-winning books:* Slaves Without Masters: The Free Negro in the Antebellum South *(1975),* Many Thousands Gone: The First Two Centuries of Slavery in Mainland North America *(1999), and* Generations of Captivity: A History of Slaves in the United States *(2002). Berlin's most recent book is* The Making of African America *(2010), from which the following selection is adapted. In this essay, Berlin explores the ways in which waves of immigration*

Reprinted from *Smithsonian Magazine*, February 2010. Adapted from the prologue of *The Making of African America*. Reprinted by permission of Viking Penguin, a division of Penguin Group (USA) Inc. and Sandra Dijkstra Literary Agency.

from Africa and the Caribbean have expanded the definition of the term "African-American," which no longer refers exclusively to descendants of slaves.

1 Some years ago, I was interviewed on public radio about the meaning of the Emancipation Proclamation. I addressed the familiar themes of the origins of that great document: the changing nature of the Civil War, the Union army's growing dependence on black labor, the intensifying opposition to slavery in the North and the interplay of military necessity and abolitionist idealism. I recalled the longstanding debate over the role of Abraham Lincoln, the Radicals in Congress, abolitionists in the North, the Union army in the field and slaves on the plantations of the South in the destruction of slavery and in the authorship of legal freedom. And I stated my long-held position that slaves played a critical role in securing their own freedom. The controversy over what was sometimes called "self-emancipation" had generated great heat among historians, and it still had life. 1

As I left the broadcast booth, a knot of black men and women—most of them technicians at the station—were talking about emancipation and its meaning. Once I was drawn into their discussion, I was surprised to learn that no one in the group was descended from anyone who had been freed by the proclamation or any other Civil War measure. Two had been born in Haiti, one in Jamaica, one in Britain, two in Ghana, and one, I believe, in Somalia. Others may have been the children of immigrants. While they seemed impressed—but not surprised—that slaves had played a part in breaking their own chains, and were interested in the events that had brought Lincoln to his decision during the summer of 1862, they insisted it had nothing to do with them. Simply put, it was not their history.

The conversation weighed upon me as I left the studio, and it has since. Much of the collective consciousness of black people in mainland North America—the belief of individual men and women that their own fate was linked to that of the group—has long been articulated through a common history, indeed a particular history: centuries of enslavement, freedom in the course of the Civil War, a great promise made amid the political turmoil of Reconstruction and a great promise broken, followed by disfranchisement, segregation and, finally, the long struggle for equality.

In commemorating this history—whether on Martin Luther King Jr.'s birthday, during Black History Month or as current events warrant—African-Americans have rightly laid claim to a unique identity. Such celebrations—their memorialization of the past—are no different from those attached to the rituals of Vietnamese Tet celebrations or the Eastern Orthodox Nativity Fast, or the celebration of the birthdays of Christopher Columbus or Casimir Pulaski; social identity is ever rooted in history. But for African-Americans, their history has always been especially important because they were long denied a past.

And so the "not my history" disclaimer by people of African descent seemed particularly pointed—enough to compel me to look closely at how previous waves of black immigrants had addressed the connections between the history they carried from the Old World and the history they inherited in the New.

In 1965, Congress passed the Voting Rights Act, which became a critical marker in African-American history. Given opportunity, black Americans voted and stood for office in numbers not seen since the collapse of Reconstruction almost 100 years earlier. They soon occupied positions that had been the exclusive preserve of white men for more than half a century. By the beginning of the 21st century, black men and women had taken seats in the United States Senate and House of Representatives, as well as in state houses and municipalities throughout the nation. In 2009, a black man assumed the presidency of the United States. African-American life had been transformed.

Within months of passing the Voting Rights Act, Congress passed a new immigration law, replacing the Johnson-Reed Act of 1924, which had favored the admission of northern Europeans, with the Immigration and Nationality Act. The new law scrapped the rule of national origins and enshrined a first-come, first-served principle that made allowances for the recruitment of needed skills and the unification of divided families.

This was a radical change in policy, but few people expected it to have much practical effect. It "is not a revolutionary bill," President Lyndon Johnson intoned. "It does not affect the lives of millions. It will not reshape the structure of our daily lives."

But it has had a profound impact on American life. At the time it was passed, the foreign-born proportion of the American population had fallen to historic lows—about 5 percent—in large measure because of the old immigration restrictions. Not since the 1830s had the foreign-born made up such a tiny proportion of the American people. By 1965, the United States was no longer a nation of immigrants.

During the next four decades, forces set in motion by the Immigration and Nationality Act changed that. The number of immigrants entering the United States legally rose sharply, from some 3.3 million in the 1960s to 4.5 million in the 1970s. During the 1980s, a record 7.3 million people of foreign birth came legally to the United States to live. In the last third of the 20th century, America's legally recognized foreign-born population tripled in size, equal to more than one American in ten. By the beginning of the 21st century, the United States was accepting foreign-born people at rates higher than at any time since the 1850s. The number of illegal immigrants added yet more to the total, as the United States was transformed into an immigrant society once again.

Black America was similarly transformed. Before 1965, black people of foreign birth residing in the United States were nearly invisible. According to the 1960 census, their percentage of the population was to the right of the decimal point. But after 1965, men and women of African descent entered the United States in ever-increasing numbers. During the 1990s, some 900,000 black immigrants came from the Caribbean; another 400,000 came from Africa; still others came from Europe and the Pacific rim. By the beginning of the 21st century, more people had come from Africa to live in the United States than during the centuries of the slave trade. At that point, nearly one in ten black Americans was an immigrant or the child of an immigrant.

African-American society has begun to reflect this change. In New York, the Roman Catholic diocese has added masses in Ashanti and Fante, while black men and women from various Caribbean islands march in the West Indian-American Carnival and the Dominican Day Parade. In Chicago, Cameroonians celebrate their nation's independence day, while the DuSable Museum of African American History hosts a Nigerian Festival. Black immigrants have joined groups such as the Egbe Omo Yoruba (National Association of Yoruba Descendants in North America), the Association des Sénégalais d'Amérique and the Fédération des Association Régionales Haïtiennes à l'Étranger rather than the NAACP or the Urban League.

To many of these men and women, Juneteenth celebrations—the commemoration of the end of slavery in the United States—are at best an afterthought. The new arrivals frequently echo the words of the men and women I met outside the radio broadcast booth. Some have struggled over the very appellation "African-American," either shunning it—declaring themselves, for instance, Jamaican-Americans or Nigerian-Americans—or denying native black Americans' claim to it on the ground that most of them had never been to Africa. At the same time, some old-time black residents refuse to recognize the new arrivals as true African-Americans. "I am African and I am an American citizen; am I not African-American?" a dark-skinned, Ethiopian-born Abdulaziz Kamus asked at a community meeting in suburban Maryland in 2004. To his surprise and dismay, the overwhelmingly black audience responded no. Such discord over the meaning of the African-American experience and who is (and isn't) part of it is not new, but of late has grown more intense.

After devoting more than 30 years of my career as a historian to the study of the American past, I've concluded that African-American history might best be viewed as a series of great migrations, during which immigrants—at first forced and then free—transformed an alien place into a home, becoming deeply rooted in a land that once was foreign, even despised. After each migration, the newcomers created new understandings of the African-American experience and new definitions of blackness. Given the numbers of black immigrants arriving after 1965, and the diversity of their origins, it should be no surprise that the overarching narrative of African-American history has become a subject of contention.

That narrative, encapsulated in the title of John Hope Franklin's classic text *From Slavery to Freedom*, has been reflected in everything from spirituals to sermons, from fold tales to TV docudramas. Like Booker T. Washington's *Up from Slavery*, Alex Haley's *Roots* and Martin Luther King Jr.'s "I Have a Dream" speech, it retells the nightmare of enslavement, the exhilaration of emancipation, the betrayal of Reconstruction, the ordeal of disfranchisement and segregation, and the pervasive, omnipresent discrimination, along with the heroic and ultimately triumphant struggle against second-class citizenship.

This narrative retains incalculable value. It reminds men and women that a shared past binds them together, even when distance and different circumstances and experiences create diverse interests. It also integrates black people's history into an American story of seemingly inevitable progress. While recognizing the realities of black poverty and inequality, it nevertheless depicts the trajectory of black life moving along what Dr. King referred to as the "arc of justice," in which exploitation and coercion yield, reluctantly but inexorably, to fairness and freedom.

Yet this story has had less direct relevance for black immigrants. Although new arrivals quickly discover the racial inequalities of American life for themselves, many—fleeing from poverty of the sort rarely experienced even by the poorest of contemporary black Americans and tyranny unknown to even the most oppressed—are quick to embrace a society that offers them opportunities unknown in their homelands. While they have subjected themselves to exploitation by working long hours for little compensation and underconsuming to save for the future (just as their native-born counterparts have done), they often ignore the connection between their own travails and those of previous generations of African-Americans. But those travails are connected, for the migrations that are currently transforming African-American life are directly connected to those that have transformed black life in the past. The trans-Atlantic passage to the tobacco and rice plantations of the coastal South, the 19th-century movement to the cotton and sugar plantations of the Southern interior, the 20th-century shift to the industrializing cities of the North and the waves of arrivals after 1965 all reflect the changing demands of global capitalism and its appetite for labor.

New circumstances, it seems, require a new narrative. But it need not—and should not—deny or contradict the slavery-to-freedom story. As the more recent arrivals add their own chapters, the themes derived from these various migrations, both forced and free, grow in significance. They allow us to see the African-American experience afresh and sharpen our awarness that African-American history is, in the end, of one piece.

We Are All Works in Progress (1998)

Leslie Feinberg

The sight of pink-blue gender-coded infant outfits may grate on your nerves. Or you may be a woman or a man who feels at home in those categories. Trans liberation defends you both.

Each person should have the right to choose between pink or blue tinted gender categories, as well as all the other hues of the palette. At this moment in time, that right is denied to us. But together, we could make it a reality....

I am a human being who would rather not be addressed as Ms. or Mr., ma'am or sir. I prefer to use gender-neutral pronouns like *sie* (pronounced like "*see*") and *hir* (pronounced like "*here*") to describe myself. I am a person who faces almost insurmountable difficulty when instructed to check off an "F" or an "M" box on identification papers.

I'm not at odds with the fact that I was born female-bodied. Nor do I identify as an intermediate sex. I simply do not fit the prevalent Western concepts of what a woman or man "should" look like. And that reality has dramatically directed the course of my life.

I'll give you a graphic example. From December 1995 to December 1996, I was dying of endocarditis—a bacterial infection that lodges and proliferates in the valves of the heart. A simple blood culture would have immediately exposed the root cause of my raging fevers. Eight weeks of 'round-the-clock intravenous antibiotic drips would have eradicated every last seedling of bacterium in the canals of my heart. Yet I experienced such hatred from some health practitioners that I very nearly died.

I remember late one night in December my lover and I arrived at a hospital emergency room during a snowstorm. My fever was 104 degrees and rising. My blood pressure was pounding dangerously high. The staff immediately hooked me up to monitors and worked to bring down my fever. The doctor in charge began physically examining me. When he determined that my anatomy was female, he flashed me a mean-spirited smirk. While keeping his eyes fixed on me, he approached one of the nurses, seated at a desk, and began rubbing her neck and shoulders. He talked to her about sex for a few minutes. After his pointed demonstration of "normal sexuality," he told me to get dressed and then he stormed out of the room. Still delirious, I struggled to put on my clothes and make sense of what was happening.

The doctor returned after I was dressed. He ordered me to leave the hospital and never return. I refused. I told him I wouldn't leave until he could tell me why my fever was so high. He said, "You have a fever because you are a very troubled person."

This doctor's prejudices, directed at me during a moment of catastrophic illness, could have killed me. The death certificate would have read: Endocarditis. By all rights it should have read: Bigotry.

As my partner and I sat bundled up in a cold car outside the emergency room, still reverberating from the doctor's hatred, I thought about how many people have been turned away from medical care when they were desperately ill—some because an apartheid "whites only" sign hung over the emergency room entrance, or some because their visible Kaposi's sarcoma lesions kept personnel far from their beds. I remembered how a blemish that wouldn't heal drove my mother to visit her doctor repeatedly during the 1950s. I recalled the doctor finally wrote a prescription for Valium because he decided she was a hysterical woman. When my mother finally got to specialists, they told her the cancer had already reached her brain.

Bigotry exacts its toll in flesh and blood. And left unchecked and unchallenged, prejudices create a poisonous climate for us all. Each of us has a stake in the demand that every human being has a right to a job, to shelter, to health care, to dignity, to respect.

I am very grateful to have this chance to open up a conversation with you about why it is so vital to also defend the right of individuals to express and define their sex and gender, and to control their own bodies. For me, it's a life-and-death question. But I also believe that this discussion will have great meaning for you. All your life you've heard such dogma about what it means to be a "real" woman or a "real" man. And chances are you've choked on some of it. You've balked at the idea that being a woman means having to be thin as a rail, emotionally nurturing, and an airhead when it comes to balancing her checkbook. You know in your guts that being a man has nothing to do with rippling muscles, innate courage, or knowing how to handle a chain saw. These are really caricatures. Yet these images have been drilled into us through popular culture and education over the years. And subtler, equally insidious messages lurk in the interstices of these grosser concepts. These ideas of what a "real" woman or man should be straightjacket the freedom of individual self-expression. These gender messages play on and on in a continuous loop in our brains, like commercials that can't be muted.

But in my lifetime I've also seen social upheavals challenge this sex and gender doctrine. As a child who grew up during the McCarthyite, Father-Knows-Best 1950s, and who came of age during the second wave of women's liberation in the United

States, I've seen transformations in the ways people think and talk about what it means to be a woman or a man.

Today the gains of the 1970s women's liberation movement are under siege by right-wing propagandists. But many today who are too young to remember what life was like before the women's movement need to know that this was a tremendously progressive development that won significant economic and social reforms. And this struggle by women and their allies swung human consciousness forward like a pendulum.

The movement replaced the common usage of vulgar and diminutive words to describe females with the word *woman* and infused that word with strength and pride. Women, many of them formerly isolated, were drawn together into consciousness-raising groups. Their discussions—about the root of women's oppression and how to eradicate it—resonated far beyond the rooms in which they took place. The women's liberation movement sparked a mass conversation about the systematic degradation, violence, and discrimination that women faced in this society. And this consciousness-raising changed many of the ways women and men thought about themselves and their relation to each other. In retrospect, however, we must not forget that these widespread discussions were not just organized to *talk* about oppression. They were a giant dialogue about how to take action to fight institutionalized anti-woman attitudes, rape and battering, the illegality of abortion, employment and education discrimination, and other ways women were socially and economically devalued.

This was a big step forward for humanity. And even the period of political reaction that followed has not been able to overturn all the gains made by that important social movement. Now another movement is sweeping onto the stage of history: Trans liberation. We are again raising questions about the societal treatment of people based on their sex and gender expression. This discussion will make new contributions to human consciousness. And trans communities, like the women's movement, are carrying out these mass conversations with the goal of creating a movement capable of fighting for justice—of righting the wrongs.

We are a movement of masculine females and feminine males, cross-dressers, transsexual men and women, intersexuals born on the anatomical sweep between female and male, gender-blenders, many other sex and gender-variant people, and our significant others. All told, we expand understanding of how many ways there are to be a human being.

Our lives are proof that sex and gender are much more complex than a delivery room doctor's glance at genitals can determine, more variegated than pink or blue birth caps. We are oppressed for not fitting those narrow social norms. We are fighting back.

Our struggle will also help expose some of the harmful myths about what it means to be a woman or a man that have compartmentalized and distorted your life, as well as mine. Trans liberation has meaning for you—no matter how you define or express your sex or your gender.

If you are a trans person, you face horrendous social punishments—from institutionalization to gang rape, from beatings to denial of child visitation. This oppression is faced, in varying degrees, by all who march under the banner of trans liberation. This brutalization and degradation strips us of what we could achieve with our individual lifetimes.

And if you do not identify as transgender or transsexual or intersexual, your life is diminished by our oppression as well. Your own choices as a man or a woman are sharply curtailed. Your individual journey to express yourself is shunted into one of two deeply carved ruts, and the social baggage you are handed is already packed.

So the defense of each individual's right to control their own body, and to explore the path of self-expression, enhances your own freedom to discover more about yourself and your potentialities. This movement will give you more room to breathe—to be yourself. To discover on a deeper level what it means to be yourself.

Together, I believe we can forge a coalition that can fight on behalf of your oppression as well as mine. Together, we can raise each other's grievances and win the kind of significant change we all long for. But the foundation of unity is understanding. So let me begin by telling you a little bit about myself.

I am a human being who unnerves some people. As they look at me, they see a kaleidoscope of characteristics they associate with both males and females. I appear to be a tangled knot of gender contradictions. So they feverishly press the question on me: woman or man? Those are the only two words most people have as tools to shape their question.

"Which sex are you?" I understand their question. It sounds so simple. And I'd like to offer them a simple resolution. But merely answering woman or man will not bring relief to the questioner. As long as people try to bring me into focus using only those two lenses, I will always appear to be an enigma.

The truth is I'm no mystery. I'm a female who is more masculine than those prominently portrayed in mass culture. Millions of females and millions of males in this country do not fit the cramped compartments of gender that we have been taught are "natural" and "normal." For many of us, the words *woman* or *man*, *ma'am* or *sir*, *she* or *he*—in and of themselves—do not total up the sum of our identities or of our oppressions. Speaking for myself, my life only comes into focus when the word *transgender* is added to the equation.

Simply answering whether I was born female or male will not solve the conundrum. Before I can even begin to respond to the question of my own birth sex, I feel it's important to challenge the assumptions that the answer is always as simple as either-or. I believe we need to take a critical look at the assumption that is built into the seemingly innocent question: "What a beautiful baby—is it a boy or a girl?"

The human anatomical spectrum can't be understood, let alone appreciated, as long as female or male are considered to be all that exists. "Is it a boy or a girl?" Those are the only two categories allowed on birth certificates.

But this either-or leaves no room for intersexual people, born between the poles of female and male. Human anatomy continues to burst the confines of the contemporary concept that nature delivers all babies on two unrelated conveyor belts. So are the birth certificates changed to reflect human anatomy? No, the U.S. medical establishment hormonally molds and shapes and surgically hacks away at the exquisite complexities of intersexual infants until they neatly fit one category or the other.

A surgeon decides whether a clitoris is "too large" or a penis is "too small." That's a highly subjective decision for anyone to make about another person's body. Especially when the person making the arbitrary decision is scrubbed up for surgery! And what is the criterion for a penis being "too small"? Too small for successful heterosexual intercourse. Intersexual infants are already being tailored for their sexuality, as well as their sex. The infants have no say over what happens to their bodies. Clearly the struggle against genital mutilation must begin here, within the borders of the United States.

But the question asked of all new parents: "Is it a boy or a girl?" is not such a simple question when transsexuality is taken into account, either. Legions of out-and-proud transsexual men and women demonstrate that individuals have a deep, developed, and valid sense of their own sex that does not always correspond to the cursory decision made by a delivery-room obstetrician. Nor is transsexuality a recent phenomenon. People have undergone social sex reassignment and surgical and hormonal sex changes throughout the breadth of oral and recorded human history.

Having offered this view of the complexities and limitations of birth classification, I have no hesitancy in saying I was born female. But that answer doesn't clear up the confusion that drives some people to ask me, "Are you a man or a woman?" The problem is that they are trying to understand my gender expression by determining my sex—and therein lies the rub! Just as most of us grew up with only the concepts of woman and man the terms feminine and masculine are the only two tools most people have to talk about the complexities of gender expression.

That pink-blue dogma assumes that biology steers our social destiny. We have been taught that being born female or male will determine how we will dress and walk, whether we will prefer our hair shortly cropped or long and flowing, whether we will be emotionally nurturing or repressed. According to this way of thinking, masculine females are trying to look "like men," and feminine males are trying to act "like women."

But those of us who transgress those gender assumptions also shatter their inflexibility.

So, why do I sometimes describe myself as a masculine female? Isn't each of those concepts very limiting? Yes. But placing the two words together is incendiary, exploding the belief that gender expression is linked to birth sex like horse and carriage. It is the social contradiction missing from Dick-and-Jane textbook education.

I actually chafe at describing myself as masculine. For one thing, masculinity is such an expansive territory, encompassing boundaries of nationality, race, and class. Most importantly, individuals blaze their own trails across this landscape.

And it's hard for me to label the intricate matrix of my gender as simply masculine. To me, branding individual self-expression as simply feminine or masculine is like asking poets: Do you write in English or Spanish? The question leaves out the possibilities that the poetry is woven in Cantonese or Ladino, Swahili or Arabic. The question deals only with the system of language that the poet has been taught. It ignores the words each writer hauls up, hand over hand, from a common well. The music words make when finding themselves next to each other for the first time. The silences echoing in the space between ideas. The powerful winds of passion and belief that move the poet to write.

That is why I do not hold the view that gender is simply a social construct—one of two languages that we learn by rote from early age. To me, gender is the poetry each of us makes out of the language we are taught. When I walk through the anthology of the world, I see individuals express their gender in exquisitely complex and ever-changing ways, despite the laws of pentameter.

So how can gender expression be mandated by edict and enforced by law? Isn't that like trying to handcuff a pool of mercury? It's true that human self-expression is diverse and is often expressed in ambiguous or contradictory ways. And what degree of gender expression is considered "acceptable" can depend on your social situation, your race and nationality, your class, and whether you live in an urban or rural environment.

But no one can deny that rigid gender education begins early on in life—from pink and blue color-coding of infant outfits to gender-labeling toys and games. And those who overstep these arbitrary borders are punished. Severely. When the steel handcuffs tighten, it is human bones that crack. No one knows how many trans lives have been lost to police brutality and street-corner bashing. The lives of trans people are so depreciated in this society that many murders go unreported. And those of us who have survived are deeply scarred by daily run-ins with hate, discrimination, and violence.

Trans people are still literally social outlaws. And that's why I am willing at times, publicly, to reduce the totality of my self-expression to descriptions like masculine female, butch, bull dagger, drag king, cross-dresser. These terms describe outlaw status. And I hold my head up proudly in that police lineup. The word *outlaw* is not hyperbolic. I have been locked up in jail by cops because I was wearing a suit and tie. Was my clothing really a crime? Is it a "man's" suit if I am wearing it? At what point—from field to rack—is fiber assigned a sex?

The reality of why I was arrested was as cold as the cell's cement floor: I am considered a masculine female. That's a *gender* violation. My feminine drag queen sisters were in nearby cells, busted for wearing "women's" clothing. The cells that we were thrown into had the same design of bars and concrete. But when we—gay drag kings and drag queens—were thrown into them, the cops referred to the cells as bull's tanks and queen's tanks. The cells were named after our crimes: gender transgression. Actual statutes against cross-dressing and cross-gendered behavior still exist in written laws today. But even where the laws are not written down, police, judges, and prison guards are empowered to carry out merciless punishment for sex and gender "difference."

I believe we need to sharpen our view of how repression by the police, courts, and prisons, as well as all forms of racism and bigotry, operates as gears in the machinery of the economic and social system that governs our lives. As all those who have the least to lose from changing this system get together and examine these social questions, we can separate the wheat of truths from the chaff of old lies. Historic tasks are revealed that beckon us to take a stand and to take action.

That moment is now. And so this conversation with you takes place with the momentum of struggle behind it.

What will it take to put a halt to "legal" and extralegal violence against trans people? How can we strike the unjust and absurd laws mandating dress and behavior for females and males from the books? How can we weed out all the forms of transphobic and gender-phobic discrimination?

Where does the struggle for sex and gender liberation fit in relation to other movements for economic and social equality? How can we reach a point where we appreciate each other's differences, not just tolerate them? How can we tear down the electrified barbed wire that has been placed between us to keep us separated, fearful and pitted against each other? How can we forge a movement that can bring about profound and lasting change—a movement capable of transforming society?

These questions can only be answered when we begin to organize together, ready to struggle on each other's behalf. Understanding each other will compel us as honest, caring people to fight each other's oppression as though it was our own.

Leslie Feinberg is a novelist, historian, and transgender activist. Her most recent book is Transgender Liberation: A movement whose time has come. Her acclaimed novel, Stone Butch Blues, won the Lambda literary award. Feinberg has also received an American Library Association Award for Gay and Lesbian Literature.

from Chapter I: Of Our Spiritual Strivings *The Souls of Black Folk*

W.E.B. Du Bois (1868–1963)

BETWEEN me and the other world there is ever an unasked question: unasked by some through feelings of delicacy; by others through the difficulty of rightly framing it. All, nevertheless, flutter round it. They approach me in a half-hesitant sort of way, eye me curiously or compassionately, and then, instead of saying directly, How does it feel to be a problem? they say, I know an excellent colored man in my town; or, I fought at Mechanicsville; or, Do not these Southern outrages make your blood boil? At these I smile, or am interested, or reduce the boiling to a simmer, as the occasion may require. To the real question, How does it feel to be a problem? I answer seldom a word.

And yet, being a problem is a strange experience,—peculiar even for one who has never been anything else, save perhaps in babyhood and in Europe. It is in the early days of rollicking boyhood that the revelation first bursts upon one, all in a day, as it were. I remember well when the shadow swept across me. I was a little thing, away up in the hills of New England, where the dark Housatonic winds between Hoosac and Taghkanic to the sea. In a wee wooden schoolhouse, something put it into the boys' and girls' heads to buy gorgeous visiting-cards—ten cents a package—and exchange. The exchange was merry, till one girl, a tall newcomer, refused my card,—refused it peremptorily, with a glance. Then it dawned upon me with a certain suddenness that I was different from the others; or like, mayhap, in heart and life and longing, but shut out from their world by a vast veil. I had thereafter no desire to tear down that veil, to creep through; I held all beyond it in common contempt, and lived above it in a region of blue sky and great wandering shadows. That sky was bluest when I could beat my mates at examination-time, or beat them at a foot-race, or even beat their stringy heads. Alas, with the years all this fine contempt began to fade; for the worlds I longed for, and all their dazzling opportunities, were theirs, not mine. But they should not keep these prizes, I said; some, all, I would wrest from them. Just how I would do it I could never decide: by reading law, by healing the sick, by telling the wonderful tales that swam in my head,—some way. With other black boys the strife was not so fiercely sunny: their youth shrunk into tasteless sycophancy, or into silent hatred of the pale world about them and mocking distrust of everything white; or wasted itself in a bitter cry, Why did God make me an outcast and a stranger in mine own house? The shades of the prison-house closed round about us all: walls strait and stubborn to the whitest, but relentlessly narrow, tall, and unscalable to sons of night who must plod darkly on in resignation, or beat unavailing palms against the stone, or steadily, half hopelessly, watch the streak of blue above.

After the Egyptian and Indian, the Greek and Roman, the Teuton and Mongolian, the Negro is a sort of seventh son, born with a veil, and gifted with second-sight in this American world,—a world which yields him no true self-consciousness, but only lets him see himself through the revelation of the other world. It is a peculiar sensation, this double-consciousness, this sense of always looking at one's self through the eyes of others, of measuring one's soul by the tape of a world that looks on in amused contempt and pity. One ever feels his two-ness,—an American, a Negro; two souls, two thoughts, two unreconciled strivings; two warring ideals in one dark body, whose dogged strength alone keeps it from being torn asunder.

From the Margins to Mainstream: The Political Power of Hip-Hop

Katina R. Stapleton

Katina R. Stapleton was born in Baltimore, Maryland in 1973. She was graduated in 1995 from the University of Maryland at College Park with a BA in print journalism and entered Duke University's political science department, where she is currently working on a dissertation that examines the role of the media in the urban education policy process. She writes and teaches on the politics of music. In this 1998 article, she describes the musical phenomenon called hip-hop in relation to African-American and youth culture, demonstrating the relationship between music and political action.

1 'They didn't know what they were playing with, look what they got', spoke Jungle Brothers rapper Mike G from the floor of a conference on the state of hip-hop in the late 1990s. In the 20-plus years since it emerged in inner-city New York as an alternative to violence and a way to escape harsh urban realities, hip-hop has become a worldwide musical and cultural force. But the widespread popularity of rap music and hip-hop culture among youth has caught many outside the hip-hop community by surprise. Once considered 'black noise', hip-hop has claimed for itself the role of cultural and political voice of an entire generation of youth.

When hip-hop emerged in New York City in the 1970s, its primary sphere of influence was the youth in the neighborhoods where

---

it evolved. In areas like the Bronx, breakdancers, graffiti artists, MCs (rappers), DJs and fans formed the hip-hop community. Hip-hop scholar Tricia Rose argues that 'alternative local identities were forged in fashions and language, street names, and most important, in establishing neighborhood crews or posses' (Rose, 1994: 34). Crews provided an opportunity for youth to form family-like bonds similar to, but not based on, gang affiliation. Instead of always fighting with fists, hip-hop gave youth the option of fighting with words, art, dance or the ability to produce good beats (Fernando, 1994).

Hip-hop emerged at a time of crisis for youth in urban communities. The situation was no less than a 'deindustrialized meltdown where social alienation, prophetic imagination, and yearning intersect' (Rose, 1994: 21). Hip-hop enabled youth to create their own cultural space within the city that countered the poverty and alienation that surrounded them on a day-to-day basis. As a type of genuine street culture, hip-hop evolved for several years before being discovered by the mass media (Shomari, 1995).

As scholars began to research hip-hop, it became clear that while it developed as an alternative youth culture, hip-hop incorporated many elements of the larger African-American and African cultures (DeMott, 1988; Floyd, 1995; Remes, 1991; Stephens, 1991). One such element is 'playing the dozens', a time-honored tradition in the African-American community. Also known as bragging, boasting, toasting or signifying, the process includes 'ritual insults' in which the speakers test their verbal prowess by seeing who can form the best taunt. Dozens-playing was an integral part of the early rap competitions and has remained a significant element of rap music today.

Hip-hop's use of the spoken or sung word to tell stories and teach 'life-lessons' is also part of a tradition among African peoples that goes back to the *griots*, African storytellers who played the important role of oral historians. The griots' role in African communities was to pass down the stories of each generation in song, while imparting knowledge about society. 'Endowed with this much prized oral skill, the griot enjoyed a very respected position within his community, just like many modern-day microphone personalities' (Fernando, 1994: 255). Rappers have become urban griots, using their lyrics to disperse social commentary about what it means to be young and black in the late 20th century (Kuwahara, 1992).

Like more traditional griots, what makes hip-hop artists such successful purveyors of cultural and political information is that they relay messages of importance to youth in a form that they enjoy. Rap music, currently the most visible element of hip-hop, has proven its ability to both capture the ear of those who listen to it for aesthetic reasons and those who look to the genre for deeper meaning. From its rough and tumble forms to the most commercial jams, hip-hop has been able to raise awareness among African-Americans and the general public about the issues that face black youth on a day-to-day basis.

Another strong tradition in African-American music that hip-hop has followed is the use of song to 'tell it like it is' and protest against social injustice (Nelson, 1992; Remes, 1991). In the early 1900s an examination of Negro spirituals as folksongs noted that folksongs were developed out of experience (Krehbiel, 1914). The pathos of what it meant to be a slave was reflected in music of the times. Krehbiel writes, 'as a rule the finest songs are the fruits of suffering undergone and the hope of deliverance from bondage' (Krehbiel, 1914: 26–7). Rochelle Larking (1972) argues that the historic conditions of black Americans will always serve as a basis for protest music. Her 1970s examination of soul music as a form of protest noted that beginning with the blues, black popular music has joined church songs as calls to freedom.

African-Americans, according to the musicologist Jon Spencer, have used secular music such as the blues to reflect the 'hell on earth' which they have been subjected to throughout the ages. These songs, claims Spencer, are no less profound than Old Testament psalms and lamentations. Like these biblical tales of woe, the blues are songs 'that reveal the nitty-gritty details of life as it is lived at the underside of society and the underbelly of history' (Spencer, 1996: xiv). Black music from the blues to funk, soul, jazz and now to hip-hop often shares the hope for deliverance found in Negro folksongs. As noted by Henry Charles (1990), the concept of deliverance is found in many aspects of African-American culture.

The central purpose of this article is to examine how hip-hop culture and music are uniquely situated among youth as a means of political action. While the most obvious means is through lyrical protest, Mark Mattern (1997) provides a larger framework for political action that includes music and the culture in which it develops. In his examination of Cajun music, Mattern suggests three categories of political action that will also form the basis of my analysis: confrontational (protest), deliberative and pragmatic.

Hidden transcripts and confrontational lyrics

> Creating culture is not easy. . . . There is a politically conscious, culturally aware, liberated, Black survival kit side to rap music that is being seriously overlooked. (Jackson, 1994)

One of the greatest contributions of hip-hop artists to the political landscape is one of protest. Mattern (1997) argues that the use of music to provide protest is a clear example of confrontational political action. Protest music is characterized by objections to injustices and oppressions inflicted on certain individuals and groups. Resistance is key and so are clear distinctions between those being subjugated and those perpetrating the injustice. 'Typically, the intent of protest musicians is to oppose the exploitation and oppression exercised by dominant elites and members of dominant groups' (Mattern, 1997: 2). Mattern finds similar elements of resistance in Cajun music that had been previously found in rap music.

In her seminal study of hip-hop, Tricia Rose (1994) provides an examination of rap music and hip-hop culture as a means to resist the dominant social order. Drawing on the work of James Scott (1990), Rose makes the critical distinction between the means by which those in dominant versus marginalized groups are able to get their messages across. Those in power are represented by dominant public transcripts, which are 'maintained through a wide range of social practices', such as setting the terms of public debate (Rose, 1994: 100). Cut out of the public debate, marginalized groups develop their own resistive or hidden transcripts. These communications take place in disguised form and tend to include critiques of the predominant culture. As one of the most marginalized groups in American history, African-Americans have long fought to be included in public debate. Since its inception, one of the areas found to be most problematic for the expression of African-American culture has been television. While there has been more of an influx of television shows and films that feature African-Americans in recent years, critics argue that blacks are mostly portrayed as comedic objects or criminals (Dates and Barlow, 1990; Greenberg and Brand, 1990). Black youths in particular have looked to the media to find representations of their own lives. Rap music and rap music videos gained in popularity among black youth as they recognized rap as their voice. Rap veteran Chuck D of Public Enemy has been widely quoted as calling rap music the 'Black man's CNN'. In the face of under- and/or misrepresentation in traditional media, black youths have turned to hip-hop as a means to define themselves. In terms of resistance, hip-hop provided a forum from which black youth can portray what it means to be young and black in America and protest against it. In its musical form, hip-hop has been able to form what are termed 'hidden transcripts'. While those from dominant cultural groups have public transcripts, those from marginalized groups often must create their own forum from which they can communicate with each other and transmit messages to the dominant culture. The use of resistive transcripts in rap music serves the dual purpose of using symbolism to critique power holders (Rose, 1994) and providing a dialogic arena in which rappers shape the terms of entry (Skeggs, 1993).

The transcripts found in rap music, while often protesting the treatment of all African-Americans, find black youth, not adults, as their primary audience. Dates and Barlow (1990) suggest that this age division among African-Americans over rap is based in part on perceived class consciousness. They argue that this can be seen in radio programming. Many radio formats reflect a class style, with stations wooing urban contemporary listeners with jazz, soul and traditional R&B while other stations woo black youth with hip-hop influenced R&B and rap music (Dates and Barlow, 1990; Jackson, 1994). In terms of political action, this means that black youth and black adults are finding that they have differing ideas of what protest music should sound like. While 'Say it Loud, I'm Black and I'm Proud' by James Brown and 'Respect' by Aretha Franklin were anthems for blacks who came of age in the 1960s, rap is providing new anthems for black youth of the 1990s.

One of the earliest raps credited with going beyond the boast/party elements of rap music to provide a protest anthem was simply called 'The Message'. Released by Grandmaster Flash and the Furious Five in the early 1980s, 'The Message' captured the angst of black youth growing up in the inner city and lent its name to a type of rap music that would follow.

Flash's message that society shouldn't push him because he was close to the edge was something that anyone who had grown up in the ghetto could understand. According to Flash, being raised in the impoverished 'second rate' conditions is what often causes young blacks to harbor deep feelings of anger towards society.

While raps like 'The Message' may have started with GrandMaster Flash in 1982, over the years, the group Public Enemy has brought hard-hitting societal critiques to the forefront of hip-hop. Public Enemy has brought hard-hitting societal critiques to the forefront of hip-hop. Public Enemy's founder and lead rapper Chuck D, writes how PE decided to use their music for social purposes:

> The sociopolitical meaning of Public Enemy came after we decided the group would be called that, because the meaning and the connection of what we were about fit right in. The Black man and woman was considered three-fifths of human being in the Constitution of the United States. Since the government and the general public follow the Constitution, then we must be the enemy. (Chuck D, 1997: 86)

Public Enemy credit their strong commitment to protest to the influences of the Black Panther Party and the Nation of Islam. The combination of PE's political background and their ability to create strong musical and video images allowed them to use their songs to provide powerful statements. Two of the most remembered rap commentaries from PE are '911 is a Joke' and 'Fight the Power'. Even before newspaper and television reporters started telling the general public about the problems inner-city residents had with receiving prompt ambulance service, Public Enemy detailed the situation in rhyme. The raps of nationalist groups such as Public Enemy serve as direct examples of confrontational political action. One criterion of this type of political action is the placement of the group, which is perceived as being oppressed in direct opposition to the oppressors (Mattern, 1997). The resistive transcripts of Public Enemy's song 'Hitler Day', locate people of color in direct opposition to white America.

'Hitler Day' is a critique of America's celebration of Columbus Day. According to the rap, a holiday which celebrates the 'discovery' of America at the expense of its native inhabitants is inherently offensive to people of color.

Chuck D explains that asking native and African-American people to celebrate Columbus Day is analogous to asking Jews to celebrate Adolf Hitler Day. 'For me, that's what Christopher Columbus represents to Black, Brown, and Red nations in North America and throughout the world because he opened the gates for five hundred years of mayhem' (Chuck D, 1997: 198). Other more well known confrontational songs by the group include 'Shut 'Em Down', which encouraged the boycotting of businesses that take from the black community without giving back, and the self-explanatory rap 'Fight the Power'.

Other nation-conscious rappers like Brand-Nubian, X-Clan, Poor Righteous Teachers and KRS-One have provided either direct indictments of the dominant social structure or more hidden critiques (Decker, 1993; Eurie and Spady, 1991; Henderson, 1996). But nation-consciousness in rap music also includes messages of empowerment. Next to Public Enemy, Kris Parker is one of the most well known deliverers of political and social messages to the hip-hop community. Ironically, Kris Parker (KRS-One) began his career as part of Boogie Down Productions (BDP) with the late Scott LaRock. Posing on the cover of 'Criminal Minded with Guns', BDP produced some of the earliest music with a gangster ethic, while at the same time promoting messages of black nationalism, safe sex and the rejection of the drug trade. As a solo artist, KRS-One has cemented his role as a teacher among the hip-hop community. From his 1997 album *I Got Next* KRS-One urges the hip-hop nation to shed what he calls ghetto mentality for one of success. Both Public Enemy and KRS-One represent nation-consciousness based in the 1960s black power movement. Jeffery Decker contends that hip-hop nationalists:

> . . . are most effective when they appropriate popular knowledge from within the black community and exploit its most progressive elements in the process of envisioning a new society. At these moments rappers function in a manner resembling what Antonio Gramsci calls 'organic intellectuals'. (Decker, 1993: 59)

Much of the literature on the presence of confrontational political action in music is implicitly or explicitly indebted to Gramscian Marxism. Organic intellectuals are individuals who hold close ties to their class of origin and whose function is to express class identity and goals (Mattern, 1997). The relationship of the hip-hop artist to a class identity has been clear since hip-hop began. Early hip-hop artists came directly from specific inner-city communities and represented a class of youth facing economic deprivation along with social and political marginalization. Even though the hip-hop community has expanded beyond its core to include youth of all classes, races and cultures, hip-hop artists are expected to remain true to their positions as the representative of black youth. 'Hip-hop nationalists are organic cultural intellectuals to the degree that their activities are directly linked to the everyday struggles of black folk and that their music critically engages the popular knowledge of which they have a part' (Decker, 1993: 59). Henderson (1996) and Decker (1993) note that many prominent examples of hip-hop nationalists are not explicitly linked to 1960s nationalism. The Fugees are among rappers whose vision of nationhood is bounded not by geography, but rather one's link to the African or Afro-Hispanic diaspora. Referring to black youth as black diamonds and pearls, Fugees vocalist Lauren Hill raps, 'If I ruled the world, I'd free all my sons'. This type of nationalism is Afrocentric in nature. Rappers like Queen Latifah look to Mother Africa for inspiration in forming their hip-hop identity.

Gangster rap is another prominent source of confrontational nationalist rap (Decker, 1993). Known for their universal distrust of the police, gangster rappers often use their music to provide graphic indictments of the police and the government interspersed with tales of gangster living. Many gangster rappers prefer to be called realists, because they feel their rap describes what is really going on in the 'hood. With black on black violence being the leading source of death for black youth since 1969, it doesn't seem wrong to many rappers to reflect that in their music (Kitwana, 1994: 41). King George, a member of TRU, contends that this type of realism is more than just talk about killing. 'I'm just relating to what's going on and keeping everybody aware at the same time' (Davis, 1996: 63).

Gender and gangsta-rap

Claims to realism aside, however, there has been widespread debate about whether or not songs that call black women 'bitches' and 'hoes' (whores) as well as songs which detail sex acts, drug sales and extreme violence are negative influences of youth. The portrayal of women and whites in hip-hop music have been special sources of concern (Allison, 1994; Hansen, 1995; Johnson et al., 1995). It would seem obvious that no woman would want to be called a female dog on tape, or have their boyfriends 'Treat 'em like a prostitute'. But while female rappers like M.C. Lyte, Queen Latifah, Yo-Yo and Salt 'n' Pepa began to challenge the conception that only males could rap and shape perceptions of women in the urban community, some female rappers responded by becoming hard-core rappers themselves (Rose, 1994; Skeggs, 1993)

In the late 1990s female rappers have emerged as a force equal to male rappers. Skeggs (1993) argues that if rap in general is used to combat racism and oppression, female artists use rap to battle sexism. While many female hip-hop artists rap about female solidarity, others provide images of women being in control of their sexuality. Skeggs theorizes that for black women, 'sexuality is one of the few cultural resources that they can use for the construction of embodied self worth' (Skeggs, 1993: 310). This notion has not gone unchallenged. Female rappers like Lil' Kim and Foxy Brown have been both vilified and held up for praise for their hard-core attitude and blatantly sexy style. The question 'harlots or heroines?' has followed them since they came on the scene. While supporters celebrate the two female rappers' ability to take charge and proclaim their sexuality, critics challenge their claim to feminism. The Lady of Rage, like many other female rappers, holds conflicting views of artists like Kim and Foxy. "I like Little Kim because she sounds so hard. At first I thought what she was saying was not good because we already got problems as far as women getting recognition and being accepted. I felt that might hinder it a little bit.' But, as Rage notes, 'Sex sells and she's good' (Williams, 1997:63).

Many in the hip-hop community contend that while there are valid concerns about the level of sexual and violent content in hip-hop music, the concern from the media and politicians is not genuine. In stead, negative sentiments towards hip-hop are considered to have racial overtones. Hip-hop artists in attendance at the 1997 Life After Death conference contended that the media and politicians are down on hip-hop because it is a black art from that is being consumed by white youth. The consumption of hip-hop by young whites allows them to become 'ghetto chic' without actually having to live in ghetto conditions (Allison, 1994). Though much of the criticism of hip-hop comes from those outside of the black community, there is a large concern about the tone of rap music within African-American discourse. Rose, who applauds rap for its ability to provide resistive transcripts, lambasts rappers for their sexism. 'I am thoroughly frustrated but not surprised by the apparent need for some rappers to craft elaborate and creative stories about the abuse and domination of young black women' (Rose, 1994: 15).

Likewise, trends toward the inclusion of sex, drugs, violence and, most recently, materialism in rap music have not gone unnoticed or unchallenged by member s of the hip-hop community itself (Life After Death, 1997). Hip-hop conferences held in the aftermath of the violent deaths of favorite sons, Tupac Shakur and the Notorious B.I.G. have looked at whether hip-hop has a social responsibility to the youth that listen to the music. Participants at Life After Death (1997) asked serious questions about the role of violence in the genre. The consensus among panel and audience members seemed to be that in many ways hip-hop is out of control. However, they note—and I agree—that rappers who talk about sex and violence should not be expected to take all the blame. Equal shares of blame should lie with record companies and managers who promote violent/sexual rappers, with the youth who buy these records, and with parents who do not take the time to listen to what their children are listening to. Blame also lies with American society itself, which criticizes rappers for talking about ideals that are in fact embedded in the American way of life, as well as the media who often blow up the violence in hip-hop out of context. A sampling of newspaper articles following the shooting death of Biggie Smalls seems to support claims that in a society where black men are killed in record numbers the media still insist on implying that the rap industry, not guns, kills people (Patillo, 1997).

The fact that rappers reflect aspects of American society and the pursuit of the American dream is important in a political context. Rap has many elements in common with country and hard rock music, but receives more critical attention. 'Rap and country lyrics implicate underclass reality, that the alternative symbol systems have a parallel socio-economic provenience' (Armstrong, 1993: 69). Though both genres are based on somewhat different social realities, they both share a rhetoric of violence. Analyses of press coverage of country and rap have found that while the genres share a tendency towards machismo, they are not treated the same way by the press. The difference, as found by Noe, lies not in the song lyrics, but in the racial lenses through which the songs are interpreted.

> When Ice Cube says, 'Let the suburbs see a nigga invasion', many whites interpret that as an incitement to violence. But when Johnny Cash sings, 'Shot a man in Reno/just to watch him die', the public taps its feet and hums. (Noe, 1995: 20)

The irony, says Noe, is that rap is no more amoral than other musical genres, but rappers are being punished for catering to prevalent American themes: sex, violence and materialism.

Setting the boundaries of hip-hop

Hip-hop is bigger than any one person's opinion of what it should be, said Chuck D of Public Enemy, now a reporter for the Fox News Channel (Chuck D, 1997: 152). The process of establishing where the boundaries of hip-hop should stand is one of deliberation. Mattern (1997) elaborates on this type of political action. He writes, 'Deliberation is a political process and a form of political action in its own right, as well as a necessary preliminary step in forging agreement on common interests and goals for action in other political arenas to address them' (Mattern, 1997: 7). Mattern uses rap and Cajun music as examples of how differing visions of what a genre should stand for are deliberated within a community. The main point of deliberation within the hip-hop community revolves around the question: 'Has hip-hop gone too far?' Related questions include, but are not limited to: 'Has rap music become too sexual, too violent, and too materialistic?' 'Has hip-hop sold its soul for commercial success?' 'Has hip-hop crossed too far into the territory of other music forms?' 'As a community, has hip-hop become more suburban and white than black and urban?'

The answers to all these questions are not clear-cut. The very nature of hip-hop culture has been one that accommodated many types of people, many types of subject matter, and many types of music. The underlying question, then, is whether or not hip-hop can accommodate varying interests, while still retaining its distinctive urban identity. The presence of intra-group differences and disagreements, and of border zones between different groups, suggests that we consider, at least in some instances, a framework for understanding and action of negotiation, rather than an either-or struggle between opposing forces. Popular music would be viewed in these cases as a site and a medium for disagreement and debate over both intra- and inter-group identity and commitments. This takes shape in a deliberative form of political action (Mattern, 1997:6).

Hip-hop's identity as form of resistance among black youth lies at the heart of deliberation in the hip-hop community. Part of hip-hop's credibility among young blacks lies in its ability to claim that it is an authentic street culture (Powell, 1991). But if hip-hop is 'by the ghetto, for the ghetto', how is the community changed by the fact that it is being played on college campuses across the nation and in the homes of suburban whites? When hip-hop style is being used to sell movies, breath mints, sodas, make-up, fast food, alcohol, clothing, shoes and various other products, one knows that this is a valid concern (Blair, 1993). Similar feelings have been reported from England's hip-hop community. 'Hip-hop's integrity has been prostituted in the pursuit of financial gain', writes a columnist in *Hip-Hop Connection*, one of Britain's hip-hop magazines (Salsa, 1997: 5). Though the author was from England, she accurately summed up concerns that are held across the hip-hop community. Salsa charges that hip-hop is at its best in its resistive mode, but that it has lost its subversiveness due to mainstreaming and commercialization. Bernard-Donais (1994: 133) shares this opinion. 'The very fact that it is covered by an institution like the [*New York*] *Times* suggests that rap has found its way into the canon, and that it has ceased to be the subversive (or in other terms, marginal) form that it had been at one time.'

In the case of hip-hop, the transference from subculture to mainstream has been driven by technological advances. As long as artists performed rap in venues limited to neighborhoods, its marginal status was assured. But as rap music expanded to being mass produced hip-hop spread across the nation (Blair, 1993; Kuwahara, 1992). Hip-hop's influence has not been limited to America. Fans from across the world are able to buy rap music both from traditional record stores and from mail order distribution. The worldwide audience for hip-hop should not be underestimated (Toop, 1991). Hip-hop artists regularly perform to international audiences. Wu Tang Clan and the Fugees are just two examples of what is called global hip-hop. The appeal of hip-hop around the world is based in part on the fact that marginalization, oppression and struggle can be understood by many youth. The love of hip-hop has a universal appeal, agrees Chuck D (1997). He believes that one of the reasons that rap crosses over successfully into mainstream culture is that young whites are able to gain an African-American perspective through the music.

The character of deliberation within the hip-hop community is necessarily shaped by its widespread audience. Stephens (1991) contends that rap provides a 'double-voiced discourse' in which rap crosses racial and geographic boundaries. Hip-hop, writes Stephens, provides a point of intersection where blacks and whites can have a dialogue. Though not always acknowledge in the media, the members of the Hispanic community have also been involved in hip-hop since its inception. In this case, it is urbanity and similar social situations that guide Hispanic contributions to hip-hop (Fernando, 1994; Stephens, 1991). As Rose notes, 'Rap's black cultural address and its focus on marginal identities may appear to be in opposition to its crossover appeal for people from different racial or ethnic groups and social positions', but in reality it suggests 'that rap is a black idiom that prioritizes black culture and that articulates the problems of black urban life in the face of such diverse constituencies' (Rose, 1994: 4).

Discussions of hip-hop as a street culture sometimes overlook contributions of college students who have since become hip-hop artists and the strong identification of many black college students with hip-hop culture. Music, if not social class, draws young African-Americans of differing socioeconomic status to hip-hop.

Zillman et al. have looked at the effects of popular rock, non-political rap and radical political rap on African-American and white high-school students. They found that while radical political rap seemed to motivate white students to be more supportive of racial harmony, there was no positive link between political rap and ethnic consciousness or ethnic solidarity among the black students (Zillman et al., 1995). The authors note that this does not imply that message rap does not have an effect on black students. In fact the opposite could be true.

> It can be argued that African-American students, in contrast to white students, are massively exposed to rap and that any effect of rap may have manifested itself already prior to exposure. Several additional exposures thus could have influenced white students, especially those who are relatively unfamiliar with radical rap, but not African-American students—because of the informational saturation and its perceptual and evaluative consequences. (Zillman et al., 1995: 21)

Debate about the relative effects of hip-hop on youth is a major area of discussion within the academic community. Instead of concentrating on consciousness, researchers Johnson et al. looked at the effects of violent rap on youth. They found that there was greater acceptance of dating violence among youth exposed to violent rap videos than those exposed to non-violent rap videos or no video at all. In a slightly different experiment they also found that youth exposed to either type of rap video expressed greater desire to be like the materialistic youth portrayed in a scenario than his college-bound friend (Johnson et al., 1995).

Materialism, sexism and violence are points of deliberation among hip-hop artists and fans. Chuck D (1997) recounts the extremely negative reactions he got from African hip-hop fans to the newest incarnations of hip-hop. But as he also notes, the more negative aspects of rap are the easiest to market. 'If you give a fourteen-year-old a choice between a positive video, and a video with tits and ass, or guns and violence, he's going to choose the tits and ass, guns and violence almost every time' (Chuck D, 1997: 33). Researchers have shown that white youth who listen to rap are particularly attracted to its most violent elements. 'The more rappers are packaged as violent black criminals, the bigger their audiences become', writes Ewan Allison (1994: 449).

Is this preoccupation with ghetto culture detrimental to youth, black or white? In some ways it is positive, according to Rose, because the ghetto provides a source of social identity for the millions of youth who call it home. Other positive interpretations include the fact that rap has values both because of its brutal honesty and as a point of deliberation. Freestyle rapper Supernatural feels that gangster rap gives other types of rappers more incentive to present the hip-hop experience from all points of view. Looking at the situation from a slightly different perspective, KRS-One notes that the existence of more than one type of rap exposes the tendency for the public to choose negative over positive. Among participants at Life After Death (1997), the origins of hip-hop were seen as being positive in contrast to more recent developments. Old-school hip-hop artists stressed that hip-hop has strayed too far from its original intentions of combating gang activity to promoting gangster ethics; from promoting black unity to encouraging east coast-west coast feuds; from MC'ing, DJ'ing, breaking, and painting graffiti to simply rapping; from performing for the love of it to performing for money; and from simple boasting to gross exaggerations of one's sexual prowess (Life After Death, 1997; Nia, 1997). Though each of these issues is important to the future of hip-hop, the charge that there has been a dilution of hip-hop as a distinct, protest-based culture and music form is the most political.

Actions speak louder than words

Though the previous discussion in this article has concentrated on both the resistive and deliberative aspects of hip-hop, Mattern suggests music and its related culture also can be used as a basis for pragmatic political action. This type of action, says Mattern, 'begins from the premise of shared political interests. Pragmatic political action occurs when individuals and groups use music to promote awareness of shared interests and to organize collaborative action to address them' (Mattern, 1997: 7). In the past, hip-hop artists have come together for many causes. One prominent example, though considered ill-fated, was the Stop the Violence movement (STV), an attempt to discourage black-on-black crime. Other movements include HEAL (Human Education Against Lies) and the current Rap the Vote project.

Currently there seems to be a resurgence of hip-hop artists attempting to form groups to further the common interests of African-diasporic peoples and/or members of the hip-hop nation. KRS-One, whose song 'Stop the Violence' typified the spirit of the STV movement, has recently started the Temple of Hip-Hop, a non-profit cultural center with the purpose of preserving hip-hop culture. The Zulu nation remains a long-standing conduit of nationalism within the hip-hop community. Many other rap groups and individual artists have taken on specific service projects in order to give back to the community. Perhaps some of the most interesting projects are coming from the ground up. One such project is the Wiseguys, led by Raymond 'Ray Benzino' Scott, president of Boston-based Surrender Records. Using a similar concept to the one of trading a gang for a team, Scott and three friends encouraged former gang rivals to 'trade their hardware for mics'. The project, called Wiseguys, resulted in former gang members coming together to record an album now distributed nationally. Says Scott, 'It becomes a political platform of hypocrisy when you're scared to actually go in and touch the people who are going through the problems' (Walker, 1997: 30–1).

Whether initiated by artists, producers or fans, it is clear that hip-hop has great potential for becoming a major agent of change. All hip-hop needs, according to Chuck D and others, is organization. 'We have to really tie up some areas in the hip-hop Nation: the Zulu Nation, the Rhyme Syndicate, any organization is good. It's just that we have to drop these badges when we come down to dialogue and figure out how to help our people . . .' (Chuck D, 1997: 181). Robert Jackson, author of the *The Last Black Mecca*, believes that an organized hip-hop nation has the potential to be a powerful social and political base within the African-American community: 'The next revolution should be more than televised—it should be political' (Jackson, 1994: 99). The next level for hip-hop, says Jackson, is to organize around a progressive political agenda which would include housing, education and health reform as well as affirmative action and employment.

Music has always been a major source of cultural identity within the African-American community. Rap music is no exception. As part of the larger hip-hop culture, rap music has served to form a cohesive bond among urban youth. Through the mass distribution of hip-hop records and videos, hip-hop has also been able to at least partially erase lines between young people of different socioeconomic backgrounds and vastly different geographic locations. Equally important, hip-hop culture has established itself as a powerful informational tool and means of resistance. It is not an overstatement to say that despite its faults, hip-hop has provided America with one of its only hard-hitting indictments of the social conditions that continue to be a harsh reality for African-American young people.

Hip-hop has shown itself to be both the site of political controversy and a means of more than one type of political action. As Mattern notes, confrontational, deliberative and pragmatic political action can occur 'whenever music is produced and consumed', and thus, '[they] should not be viewed as mutually exclusive of each other' (Mattern, 1997: 8). In the case of hip-hop, this is especially true. Rap music, while a significant source of political action within hip-hop, should not be considered its only source. It is its presence within hip-hop community that lends it the context in which resistance emerges. As the hip-hop community looks towards the 21st century, it will be the challenge of hip-hop to define how hip-hop will continue to evolve as a culture and as genuine political force.

References

Allison, E. (1994) 'It's a Black Thing: Hearing How Whites Can't', *Cultural Studies* 8(3): 438–56.

Armstrong, E.G. (1993) 'The Rhetoric of Violence in Rap and Country Music', *Sociological Inquiry* 63(1): 64–83.

Bernard-Donais, M. (1994) 'Jazz, Rock 'n' Roll, Rap and Politics', *Journal of Popular Culture* 28(2): 127–38.

Blair, M.E. (1993) 'The Commercialization of the Rap Music Youth Subculture', *Journal of Popular Culture* 27(3): 21–32.

Charles, H. (1990) *Culture and African American Politics.* Bloomington: Indiana University Press.

Craddock-Willis, A. (1989) 'Rap Music and the Black Musical Tradition', *Radical America* 23(4): 29–38.

D. Chuck (1997) *Fight the Power: Rap, Race and Reality.* New York: Delacorte Press.

Dates, J.L. and W. Barlow (1990) *Split Image: African Americans in the Mass Media.* Washington, DC: Howard University Press.

Davis, T. (1996) 'King George: Tru Royalty', *4080* 35: 63.

Decker, J. (1993) 'The State of Rap: Time and Place in Hip Hop Nationalism', *Social Text* 34: 53–84.

DeMott, D. (1988) 'The Future is Unwritten: Working-Class Youth Cultures in England and America', *Critical Text* 5(1): 42–56.

Eurie, J.D. and J.G. Spady (eds) (1991) *Nation Conscious Rap.* New York: PC International Press.

Fernando, S.H. (1994) *The New Beats: Exploring the Music, Culture, and Attitudes of Hip-Hop Culture.* New York: Harmony Books.

Floyd, S.A. (1995) *The Power of Black Music: Interpreting its History from Africa to the United States*. New York: Oxford University Press.

Greenberg, B. and J. Brand (1994) 'Minorities and the Mass Media: 1970s to 1990s', pp. 273–314 in J. Bryant and D. Zillman (eds) *Media Effects: Advances in Theory and Research*. Hillsdale, NJ: Lawrence Erlbaum Associates.

Hansen, C.H. (1995) 'Predicting Cognitive and Behavioral Effects of Gangsta Rap,' *Basic and Applied Social Psychology* 16(1–2): 43–52.

Henderson, E.A. (1996) 'Black Nationalism and Rap Music', *Journal of Black Studies* 26(3): 308–39.

Jackson, R. (1994) *The Last Black Mecca: Hip-Hop*. Chicago, IL: Research Associates and Frontline Distribution International Inc.

Johnson, J.D., et al. (1995) 'Violent Attitudes and Deferred Academic Aspirations: Deleterious Effects of Exposure to Rap Music', *Basic and Applied Social Psychology* 16(1–2): 27–41.

Kitwana, B. (1994) *The Rap on Gangsta Rap*. Chicago, IL: Third World Press.

Krehbiel, H.E. (1914) *Afro-American Folksongs: A Study in Racial and National Music*. New York and London: G. Shirmer.

Kuwahara, Y. (1992) 'Power to the People Y'all', *Humanity and Society* 16(1): 54–73.

Larking, R. (1972) 'The Soul Message', pp. 92–104 in R. Serge Denisoff and R. Peterson (eds) *The Sounds of Social Change*. Chicago: Rand McNally.

Life After Death: Rap, Reality and Social Responsibility (1997) Harvard University, Cambridge, MA. 3 May.

Mattern, M. (1997) 'Cajun Music, Cultural Revival: Theorizing Political Action in Popular Music', paper prepared for delivery at the 1997 Annual Meeting of the American Political Science Association, Washington, DC.

Nelson, A. (1992) 'The Persistence of Ethnicity in African American Popular Music', *Explorations in Ethnic Studies* 15(1): 47–57.

Nia, M. (1997) 'From God's to Niggas, From Queens to Bitch's: Do Rappers Have An Identity Crisis?', *Beat Down* 5(5): 20.

Noe, D. (1995) 'Parallel Worlds', *Humanist* 55(4): 20–2.

Patillo, M. (1997) 'The Public Eulogy of a Slain Rapper', *The Source* 92: 83.

Powell, C. (1991) 'Rap Music: An Education with a Beat from the Street', *Journal of Negro Education* 60(3): 245–59.

Remes, P. (1991) 'Rapping: A Sociolinguistic Study of Oral Tradition', *Anthropological Society of Oxford* 22(2): 129–49.

Rose, T. (1994) *Black Noise: Rap and Black Culture in Contemporary America.* Hanover, NH: Wesleyan University Press.

Salsa, M. (1997) 'Hard Lines', *Hip Hop Connection* 104:5.

Scott, J.C. (1990) *Domination and the Arts of Resistance: Hidden Transcripts.* New Haven, CT: Yale University Press.

Shomari, H. (1995) *From the Underground: Hip Hop Culture As An Agent of Social Change.* Fairwood, NJ: X-Factor Publications.

Skeggs, B. (1993) 'Two Minute Brother: Contestation Through Gender, "Race" and Sexuality', *Innovation* 6(3): 299–322.

Spencer, J.M. (1996) *Re-searching Black Music.* Knoxville: University of Tennessee Press.

Stephens, G. (1991) 'Rap Music's Double-Voiced Discourse', *Journal of Communication Inquiry* 15(2): 70–91.

Toop, D. (1991) *Rap Attack 2: African Rap to Global Hip Hop.* London: Serpent's Tail.

Walker, S. (1997) 'Glocks Down', *The Source* 98: 30–1.

Williams, F. (1997) 'Rage against the Machine', *The Source* 94: 63–6.

Zillman, D., et al. (1995) 'Radical Rap: Does it Further Ethnic Division?', *Basic and Applied Social Psychology* 16(1–2): 1–25.

Unit 4

Unit 4 Unsettled Voices

"Ethnic identity is twin skin to linguistic identity—I am my language," writes Gloria Anzaldua. In this unit, we will consider how language defines us, and we will explore the ways that language creates its own borders, including some and excluding others.

Mother Tongue

Amy Tan

Amy Tan was born in Oakland, California in 1952, several years after her mother and father immigrated from China. She was raised in various cities in the San Francisco Bay Area. When she was eight, her essay, "What the Library Means to Me," won first prize among elementary school participants, for which Tan received a transistor radio and publication in the local newspaper. Upon the deaths of her brother and father in 1967 and 1968 from brain tumors, the family began a haphazard journey through Europe, before settling in Montreux, Switzerland, where Tan graduated in her junior year in 1969.

For the next seven years, Tan attended five schools. She first went to Linfield College in McMinnville, Oregon, and there, on a blind date, met her future husband, Lou DeMattei. She followed him to San Jose, where she enrolled in San Jose City College. She next attended San Jose State University, and, while working two part-time jobs, she became an English honor's students and a President's Scholar, while carrying a semester course load of 21 units. In 1972 she graduated with honors, receiving a B.A. with a double major in English and Linguistics. She was awarded a scholarship to attend the Summer Linguistics Institute at the University of California, Santa Cruz. In 1973, she earned her M.A. in Linguistics, also from San Jose State University, and was then awarded a Graduate Minority Fellowship under the affirmative action program at the University of California, Berkeley, where she enrolled as a doctoral student in linguistics.

---

1 I am not a scholar of English or literature. I cannot give you much more than personal opinions on the English language and its variations in this country or others.

I am a writer. And by that definition, I am someone who has always loved language. I am fascinated by language in daily life. I spend a great deal of my time thinking about the power of language—the way it can evoke an emotion, a visual image, a complex idea, or a simple truth. Language is the tool of my trade. And I use them all—all the Englishes I grew up with.

Recently, I was made keenly aware of the different Englishes I do use. I was giving a talk to a large group of people, the same talk I had already given to half a dozen other groups. The nature of the talk was about my writing, my life, and my book, *The Joy Luck Club*. The talk was going along well enough, until I remembered one major difference that made the whole talk sound wrong. My mother was in the room. And it was perhaps the first time she had heard me give a lengthy speech, using the kind of English I have never used with her. I was saying things like, "The intersection of memory upon imagination" and "There is an aspect of my fiction that relates to thus-and-thus"—a speech filled with carefully wrought grammatical phrases, burdened, it suddenly seemed to me, with nominalized forms, past perfect tenses, conditional phrases, all the forms of standard English that I had learned in school and through books, the forms of English I did not use at home with my mother.

Just last week, I was walking down the street with my mother, and I again found myself conscious of the English I was using, and the English I do use with her. We were talking about the price of new and used furniture and I heard myself saying this: "Not waste money that way." My husband was with us as well, and he didn't notice any switch in my English. And then I realized why. It's because over the twenty years we've been together I've often used that same kind of English with him, and sometimes he even uses it with me. It has become our language of intimacy, a different sort of English that relates to family talk, the language I grew up with.

5 So you'll have some idea of what this family talk I heard sounds like, I'll quote what my mother said during a recent conversation which I videotaped and then transcribed. During this conversation, my mother was talking about a political gangster in Shanghai who had the same last name as her family's, Du, and how the gangster in his

early years wanted to be adopted by her family, which was rich by comparison. Later, the gangster became more powerful, far richer than my mother's family, and one day showed up at my mother's wedding to pay his respects. Here's what she said in part:

"Du Yusong having business like fruit stand. Like off the street kind. He is Du like Du Zong—but not Tsung-ming Island people. The local people call putong, the river east side, he belong to that side local people. That man want to ask Du Zong father take him in like become own family. Du Zong father wasn't look down on him, but didn't take seriously, until that man big like become a mafia. Now important person, very hard to inviting him. Chinese way, came only to show respect, don't stay for dinner. Respect for making big celebration, he shows up. Mean gives lots of respect. Chinese custom. Chinese social life that way. If too important won't have to stay too long. He come to my wedding. I didn't see, I heard it. I gone to boy's side, they have YMCA dinner. Chinese age I was nineteen."

You should know that my mother's expressive command of English belies how much she actually understands. She reads the *Forbes* report, listens to *Wall Street Week*, converses daily with her stockbroker, reads all of Shirley MacLaine's books with ease—all kinds of things I can't begin to understand. Yet some of my friends tell me they understand 50 percent of what my mother says. Some say they understand 80 to 90 percent. Some say they understand none of it, as if she were speaking pure Chinese. But to me, my mother's English is perfectly clear, perfectly natural. It's my mother tongue. Her language, as I hear it, is vivid, direct, full of observation and imagery. That was the language that helped shape the way I saw things, expressed things, made sense of the world.

Lately, I've been giving more thought to the kind of English my mother speaks. Like others, I have described it to people as "broken" or "fractured" English. But I wince when I say that. It has always bothered me that I can think of no way to describe it other than "broken," as if it were damaged and needed to be fixed, as if it lacked a certain wholeness and soundness. I've heard other terms used, "limited English," for example. But they seem just as bad, as if everything is limited, including people's perceptions of the limited English speaker.

I know this for a fact, because when I was growing up, my mother's "limited" English limited *my* perception of her. I was ashamed of her English. I believed that her English reflected the quality of what she had to say. That is, because she expressed them imperfectly her thoughts were imperfect. And I had plenty of empirical evidence to support me: the fact that people in department stores, at banks, and at restaurants did not take her seriously, did not give her good service, pretended not to understand her, or even acted as if they did not hear her.

10 My mother has long realized the limitations of her English as well. 10
When I was fifteen, she used to have me call people on the phone to pretend I was she. In this guise, I was forced to ask for information or even to complain and yell at people who had been rude to her. One time it was a call to her stockbroker in New York. She had cashed out her small portfolio and it just so happened we were going to go to New York the next week, our very first trip outside California. I had to get on the phone and say in an adolescent voice that was not very convincing, "This is Mrs. Tan."

And my mother was standing in the back whispering loudly, "Why he don't send me check, already two weeks late. So mad he lie to me, losing me money."

And then I said in perfect English, "Yes, I'm getting rather concerned. You had agreed to send the check two weeks ago, but it hasn't arrived."

Then she began to talk more loudly. "What he want, I come to New York tell him front of his boss, you cheating me?" And I was trying to calm her down, make her be quiet, while telling the stockbroker, "I can't tolerate any more excuses. If I don't receive the check immediately, I am going to have to speak to your manager when I'm in New York next week." And sure enough, the following week there we were in front of this astonished stockbroker, and I was sitting there red-faced and quiet, and my mother, the real Mrs. Tan, was shouting at his boss in her impeccable broken English.

We used a similar routine just five days ago, for a situation that was far less humorous. My mother had gone to the hospital for an appointment, to find out about a benign brain tumor a CAT scan had revealed a month ago. She said she had spoken very good English, her best English, no mistakes. Still, she said, the hospital did not apologize when they said they had lost the CAT scan and she had come for nothing. She said they did not seem to have any sympathy when she told them she was anxious to know the exact diagnosis, since her husband and son had both died of brain tumors. She said they would not give her any more information until the next time and she would have to make another appointment for that. So she said she would not leave until the doctor called her daughter. She wouldn't budge. And when the doctor finally called her daughter, me, who spoke in perfect English—lo and behold—we had assurances the CAT scan would be found, promises that a conference call on Monday would be held, and apologies for any suffering my mother had gone through for a most regrettable mistake.

15 I think my mother's English almost had an effect on limiting my possibilities in life as well. Sociologists and linguists probably will tell you that a person's developing language skills are more influenced by peers. But I do think that the language spoken in the family, especially in immigrant families which are more insular, plays a large role in shaping the language of the child. And I believe that it affected my results on achievement tests, IQ tests, and the SAT. While my English skills were never judged as poor, compared to math, English could not be considered my strong suit. In grade school I did moderately well, getting perhaps B's, sometimes B-pluses, in English and scoring perhaps in the sixtieth or seventieth percentile on achievement tests. But those scores were not good enough to override the opinion that my true abilities lay in math and science, because in those areas I achieved A's and scored in the ninetieth percentile or higher.

This was understandable. Math is precise, there is only one correct answer. Whereas, for me at least, the answers on English tests were always a judgment call, a matter of opinion and personal experience. Those tests were constructed around items like fill-in-the-blank sentence completion, Such as, "Even though Tom was _________, Mary thought he was _________." And the correct answer always seemed to be the most bland combinations of thoughts, for example, "Even though Tom was shy, Mary thought he was charming," with the grammatical structure "even though" limiting the correct answer to some sort of semantic opposites, so you wouldn't get answers like, Even though Tom was foolish, Mary thought he was ridiculous." Well, according to my mother, there were very few limitations as to what Tom could have been and what Mary might have thought of him. So I never did well on tests like that.

The same was true with word analogies, pairs of words in which you were supposed to find some sort of logical, semantic relationship—

for example, "*Sunset* is to *nightfall* as __________ is to __________." And here you would be presented with a list of four possible pairs, one of which showed the same kind of relationship: *red* is to *stoplight, bus* is to *arrival, chills* is to *fever, yawn* is to *boring.* Well, I could never think that way. I knew what the tests were asking, but I could not block out of my mind the images already created by the first pair, "*sunset* is to *nightfall*"—and I would see a burst of colors against a darkening sky, the moon rising, the lowering of a curtain of stars. And all the other pairs of words—red, bus, stoplight, boring—just threw up a mass of confusing images, making it impossible for me to sort out something as logical as saying: "A sunset precedes nightfall" is the same as "a chill precedes a fever." The only way I would have gotten that answer right would have been to imagine an associative situation, for example, my being disobedient and staying out past sunset, catching a chill at night, which turns into feverish pneumonia as punishment, which indeed did happen to me.

I have been thinking about all this lately, about my mother's English, about achievement tests. Because lately I've been asked, as a writer, why there are not more Asian Americans represented in American literature. Why are there few Asian Americans enrolled in creative writing programs? Why do so many Chinese students go into engineering? Well, these are broad sociological questions I can't begin to answer. But I have noticed in surveys—in fact, just last week—that Asian students, as a whole, always do significantly better on math achievement tests than in English. And this makes me think that there are other Asian American students whose English spoken in the home might also be described as "broken" or "limited." And perhaps they also have teachers who are steering them away from writing and into math and science, which is what happened to me.

Fortunately, I happen to be rebellious in nature and enjoy the challenge of disproving assumptions made about me. I became an English major my first year in college, after being enrolled as pre-med. I started writing nonfiction as a freelancer the week after I was told by my former boss that writing was my worst skill and I should hone my talents toward account management.

20 But it wasn't until 1985 that I finally began to write fiction. And 20
at first I wrote using what I thought to be wittily crafted sentences, sentences that would finally prove I had mastery over the English

language. Here's an example from the first draft of a story that later made its way into *The Joy Luck Club,* but without this line: "That was my mental quandary in its nascent state." A terrible line, which I can barely pronounce.

Fortunately, for reasons I won't get into today, I later decided I should envision a reader for the stories I would write. And the reader I decided upon was my mother, because these were stories about mothers. So with this reader in mind—and in fact she did read my early drafts—I began to write stories using all the Englishes I grew up with: the English I spoke to my mother, which for lack of a better term might be described as "simple"; the English she used with me, which for lack of a better term might be described as "broken"; my translation of her Chinese, which could certainly be described as "watered down"; and what I imagined to be her translation of her Chinese if she could speak in perfect English, her internal language, and for that I sought to preserve the essence, but neither an English nor a Chinese structure. I wanted to capture what language ability tests can never reveal: her intent, her passion, her imagery, the rhythms of her speech and the nature of her thoughts.

Apart from what any critic had to say about my writing, I knew I had succeeded where it counted when my mother finished reading my book and gave me her verdict: "So easy to read."

Silence

Maxine Hong Kingston

Maxine Hong Kingston (1940–) was born in Stockton, California. One of eight children—two born in China, Kingston and the others born in the United States—Kingston spent her youth with many Chinese immigrants. Her first language was Chinese, and she was exposed from birth to the rich oral traditions of Chinese culture. Kingston entered the University of California at Berkeley on scholarship as an engineering major, but quickly switched to English literature. She received a B. A. (1962) and a teaching certificate (1965) and spent many years teaching in Hawaii. The recipient of both the National Book Critics Circle Award and the American Book Award, Kingston has written widely on life as a Chinese-American. Her books include The Woman Warrior: Memoirs of a Girlhood Among Ghosts *(1976),* China Men (1980), and Tripmaster Monkey: His Fake Book *(1989). Kingston's works are imbued with Chinese culture and reflect the rhythm of Chinese-American speech. In this essay, Kingston contrasts her years of silence in American school with the sounds of her Chinese school, as she reveals how language and cultural differences impacted her early years.*

1 When I went to kindergarten and had to speak English for the first time, I became silent. A dumbness—a shame—still cracks my voice in two, even when I want to say "hello" casually, or ask an easy question in front of the check-out counter, or ask directions of a bus driver. I stand frozen, or I hold up the line with the complete, grammatical sentence that comes squeaking out at impossible length. "What did you say?" says the cab driver, or "Speak

up," so I have to perform again, only weaker the second time. A telephone call makes my throat bleed and takes up that day's courage. It spoils my day with self-disgust when I hear my broken voice come skittering out into the open. It makes people wince to hear it, I'm getting better, though. Recently I asked the postman for special-issue stamps; I've waited since childhood for postmen to give me some of their own accord. I am making progress, a little every day.

My silence was thickest—total—during the three years that I covered my school paintings with black paint. I painted layers of black over houses and flowers and suns, and when I drew on the blackboard, I put a layer of chalk on top. I was making a stage curtain, and it was the moment before the curtain parted or rose. The teachers called my parents to school, and I saw they had been saving my pictures, curling and cracking, all alike and black. The teachers pointed to the pictures and looked serious, talked seriously too, but my parents did not understand English. ("The parents and teachers of criminals were executed," said my father.) My parents took the pictures home. I spread them out (so black and full of possibilities) and pretended the curtains were swinging open, flying up, one after another, sunlight underneath, mighty operas.

During the first silent year I spoke to no one at school, did not ask before going to the lavatory, and flunked kindergarten. My sister also said nothing for three years, silent in the playground and silent at lunch. There were other quiet Chinese girls not of our family, but most of them got over it sooner than we did. I enjoyed the silence. At first it did not occur to me I was supposed to talk or to pass kindergarten. I talked at home and to one or two of the Chinese kids in class. I made motions and even made some jokes. I drank out of a toy saucer when the water spilled out of the cup, and everybody laughed, pointing at me, so I did it some more. I didn't know that Americans don't drink out of saucers.

I liked the Negro students (Black Ghosts) best because they laughed the loudest and talked to me as if I were a daring talker too. One of the Negro girls had her mother coil braids over her ears Shanghai-style like mine; we were Shanghai twins except that she was covered with black like my paintings. Two Negro kids enrolled in Chinese school, and the teachers gave them Chinese names. Some Negro kids walked me to school and home, protecting me from the Japanese kids, who hit me and chased me and stuck gum in my ears. The Japanese kids were noisy and tough. They appeared one day in kindergarten, released from concentration camp, which was a tic-tac-toe mark, like barbed wire, on the map.

It was when I found out I had to talk that school become a misery, that the silence became a misery. I did not speak and felt bad each time that I did not speak. I read aloud in first grade, though, and heard the barest whisper with little squeaks come out of my throat. "Louder," said the teacher, who scared the voice away again. The other Chinese girls did not talk either, so I knew the silence had to do with being a Chinese girl.

Reading out loud was easier than speaking because we did not have to make up what to say, but I stopped often, and the teacher would think I'd gone quiet again. I could not understand "I." The Chinese "I" has seven strokes, intricacies. How could the American "I," assuredly wearing a hat like the Chinese, have only three strokes, the middle so straight? Was it out of politeness that this writer left off the strokes the way a Chinese has to write her own name small and crooked? No, it was not politeness; "I" is a capital and "you" is lower-case. I stared at that middle line and waited so long for its black center to resolve into tight strokes and dots that I forgot to pronounce it. The other troublesome word was "here," no strong consonant to hang on to, and so flat, when "here" is two mountainous ideographs. The teacher, who had already told me every day how to read "I" and "here," put me in the low corner under the stairs again, where the noisy boys usually sat.

When my second grade class did a play, the whole class went to the auditorium except the Chinese girls. The teacher, lovely and Hawaiian, should have understood about us, but instead left us behind in the classroom. Our voices were too soft or nonexistent, and our parents never signed the permission slips anyway. They never signed anything unnecessary. We opened the door a crack and peeked out, but closed it again quickly. One of us (not me) won every spelling bee, though.

I remember telling the Hawaiian teacher, "We Chinese can't sing 'land where our fathers died.' " She argued with me about politics, while I meant because of curses. But how can I have that memory when I couldn't talk? My mother says that we, like the ghosts, have no memories.

After American school, we picked up our cigar boxes, in which we had arranged books, brushes, and an inkbox neatly, and went to

Chinese school, from 5:00 to 7:30 P.M. There we changed together, voices rising and failing, loud and soft, some boys shouting, everybody reading together, reciting together and not alone with one voice. When we had a memorization test, the teacher let each of us come to his desk and say the lesson to him privately, while the rest of the class practiced copying or tracing. Most of the teachers were men. The boys who were so well behaved in the American school played tricks on them and talked back to them. The girls were not mute. They screamed and yelled during recess, when there were no rules; they had fistfights. Nobody was afraid of children hurting themselves or of children hurting school property. The glass doors to the red and green balconies with the gold joy symbols were left wide open so that we could run out and climb the fire escapes. We played capture-the-flag in the auditorium, where Sun Yat-sen and Chiang Kai-shek's pictures hung at the back of the stage, the Chinese flag on their left and the American flag on their right. We climbed the teak ceremonial chairs and made flying leaps off the stage. One flag headquarters was behind the glass door and the other on stage right. Our feet drummed on the hollow stage. During recess the teachers locked themselves up in their office with the shelves of books, copybooks, inks from China. They drank tea and warmed their hands at a stove. There was no play supervision. At recess we had the school to ourselves, and also we could roam as far as we could go—downtown, Chinatown stores, home—as long as we returned before the bell rang.

10 At exactly 7:30 the teacher again picked up the brass bell that sat on his desk and swung it over our heads, while we charged down the stairs, our cheering magnified in the stairwell. Nobody had to line up.

Not all of the children who were silent at American school found voice at Chinese school. One new teacher said each of us had to get up and recite in front of the class, who was to listen. My sister and I had memorized the lesson perfectly. We said it to each other at home, one chanting, one listening. The teacher called on my sister to recite first. It was the first time a teacher had called on the second-born to go first. My sister was scared. She glanced at me and looked away; I looked down at my desk. I hoped that she could do it because if she could, then I would have to. She opened her mouth and a voice came out that wasn't a whisper, but it wasn't a proper voice either. I hoped that she would not cry, fear breaking up her voice like twigs underfoot. She sounded as if she were trying to sing through weeping and strangling. She did not pause or stop to end the embarrassment. She kept going until she said the last word, and then she sat down. When it was my turn, the same voice came out, a crippled animal running on broken legs. You could hear splinters in my voice, bones rubbing jagged against one another. I was loud, though. I was glad I didn't whisper.

How strange that the emigrant villagers are shouters, hollering face to face. My father asks, "Why is it I can hear Chinese from blocks away? Is it that I understand the language? Or is it they talk loud?" They turn the radio up full blast to hear the operas, which do not seem to hurt their ears. And they yell over the singers that wail over the drums, everybody talking at once, big arm gestures, spit flying. You can see the disgust on American faces looking at women like that. It isn't just the loudness. It is the way Chinese sounds, ching-chong ugly, to American ears, not beautiful like Japanese sayonara words with the consonants and vowels as regular as Italian. We make guttural peasant noise and have Ton Duc Thang names you can't remember. And the Chinese can't hear Americans at all; the language is too soft and western music unbearable. I've watched a Chinese audience laugh, visit, talk-story, and holler during a piano recital, as if the musician could not hear them. A Chinese-American, somebody's son, was playing Chopin, which has no punctuation, no cymbals, no gongs. Chinese piano music is five black keys. Normal Chinese women's voices are strong and bossy. We American-Chinese girls had to whisper to make ourselves American-feminine. Apparently we whispered even more softly than the Americans. Once a year the teachers referred my sister and me to speech therapy, but our voices would straighten out, unpredictably normal, for the therapists. Some of us gave up, shook our heads, and said nothing, not one word. Some of us could not even shake our heads. At times shaking my head no is more self-assertion than I can manage. Most of us eventually found some voice, however faltering. We invented an American-feminine speaking personality.

The Classroom and the Wider Culture: Identity as a Key to Learning English Composition

Fan Shen, Marquette University

One day in June 1975, when I walked into the aircraft factory where I was working as an electrician, I saw many large-letter posters on the walls and many people parading around the workshops shouting slogans like "Down with the word 'I'!" and "Trust in masses and the Party!" I then remembered that a new political campaign called "Against Individualism" was scheduled to begin that day. Ten years later, I got back my first English composition paper at the University of Nebraska-Lincoln. The professor's first comments were: "Why did you always use 'we' instead of 'I'?" and "Your paper would be stronger if you eliminated some sentences in the passive voice." The clashes between my Chinese background and the requirements of English composition had begun. At the center of this mental struggle, which has lasted several years and is still not completely over, is the prolonged, uphill battle to recapture "myself."

In this paper I will try to describe and explore this experience of reconciling my Chinese identity with an English identity dictated by the rules of English composition. I want to show how my cultural background shaped-and shapes-my approaches to my writing in English and how writing in English redefined-and redefines-my ideological and logical identities. By "ideological identity" I mean the system of values that I acquired (consciously and unconsciously) from my social and cultural background. And by "logical identity" I mean the natural (or Oriental) way I organize and express my thoughts in writing. Both had to be modified or redefined in learning English composition. Becoming aware of the process of redefinition of these different identities is a mode of learning that has helped me in my efforts to write in English, and, I hope, will be of help to teachers of English composition in this country. In presenting my case for this view, I will use examples from both my composition courses and literature courses, for I believe that writing papers for both kinds of courses contributed to the development of my "English identity." Although what I will describe is based on personal experience, many Chinese students whom I talked to said that they had had the same or similar experiences in their initial stages of learning to write in English.

Identity of the Self: Ideological and Cultural

Starting with the first English paper I wrote, I found that learning to compose in English is not an isolated classroom activity, but a social and cultural experience. The rules of English composition encapsulate values that are absent in, or sometimes contradictory to, the values of other societies (in my case, China). Therefore, learning the rules of English composition is, to a certain extent, learning the values of Anglo-American society. In writing classes in the United States I found that I had to reprogram my mind, to redefine some of the basic concepts and values that I had about myself, about society, and about the universe, values that had been imprinted and reinforced in my mind by my cultural background, and that had been part of me all my life.

Rule number one in English composition is: Be yourself. (More than one composition instructor has told me, "Just write what you think.") The values behind this rule, it seems to me, are based on the principle of protecting and promoting individuality (and private property) in this country. The instruction was probably crystal clear to students raised on these values, but, as a guideline of composition, it was not very clear or useful to me when I first heard it. First of all, the image or meaning that I attached to the word "I" or "myself' was, as I found out, different from that of my English teacher. In China, "I" is always subordinated to "We"-be it the working class, the Party, the country, or some other collective body. Both political pressure and literary tradition require that "I" be somewhat hidden or buried in writings and speeches; presenting the "self' too obviously would give people the impression of being disrespectful of the Communist Party in political writings and boastful in scholarly writings. The word "I" has often been identified with another "bad" word, "individualism," which has become a synonym for selfishness in China. For a long time the words "self" and "individualism" have had negative connotations in my mind, and the negative force of the words naturally extended to the field of literary studies. As a result, even if I had brilliant ideas, the "I" in my papers always had to show some modesty by not competing with or trying to stand above the names of ancient and modern authoritative figures. Appealing to Mao or other Marxist authorities became the required way (as well as the most "forceful" or "persuasive" way) to prove one's point in written discourse. I remember that in China I had even committed what I can call "reversed plagiarism"-here, I suppose it would be called "forgery"-when I was in middle school: willfully attributing some of my thoughts to "experts" when I needed some arguments but could not find a suitable quotation from a literary or political "giant."

Now, in America, I had to learn to accept the words "I" and "Self' as something glorious (as Whitman did), or at least something not to be ashamed of or embarrassed about. It was the first and probably biggest step I took into English composition and critical writing. Acting upon my professor's suggestion, I intentionally tried to show my "individuality" and to "glorify" "I" in my papers by using as many "I's" as possible--"I think," "I believe," "I see"--and deliberately cut out quotations from authorities. It was rather painful to hand in such "pompous" (I mean immodest) papers to my instructors. But to an extent it worked. After a while I became more comfortable with only "the shadow of myself." I felt more at ease to put down my thoughts without looking over my shoulder to worry about the attitudes of my teachers or the reactions of the Party secretaries, and to speak out as "bluntly" and "immodestly" as my American instructors demanded.

But writing many "I's" was only the beginning of the process of redefining myself. Speaking of redefining myself is, in an important sense, speaking of redefining the word "I." By such a redefinition I mean not only the change in how I envisioned myself, but also the change in how I perceived the world. The old "I" used to embody only one set of values, but now it had to embody multiple sets of values. To be truly "myself," which I knew was a key to my success in learning English composition, meant not to be my Chinese self at all. That is to say, when I write in English I have to wrestle with and abandon (at least temporarily) the whole system of ideology which previously defined me in myself. I had to forget Marxist doctrines (even though I do not see myself as a Marxist by choice) and the Party lines imprinted in my mind and familiarize myself with a system of capitalist/bourgeois values. I had to put aside an ideology of collectivism and adopt the values of individualism. In composition as well as in literature classes, I had to make a fundamental adjustment: if I used to examine society and literary materials through the microscopes of Marxist dialectical materialism and historical materialism, I now had to learn to look through the microscopes the other way around, i.e., to learn to look at and understand the world from the point of view of "idealism." (I must add here that there are American professors who use a Marxist approach in their teaching.)

The word "idealism," which affects my view of both myself and the universe, is loaded with social connotations, and can serve as a good example of how redefining a key word can be a pivotal part of redefining my ideological identity as a whole.

To me, idealism is the philosophical foundation of the dictum of English composition: "Be yourself." In order to write good English, I knew that I had to be myself, which actually meant not to be my Chinese self. It meant that I had to create an English self and be that self. And to be that English self, I felt, I had to understand and accept idealism the way a Westerner does. That is to say, I had to accept the way a Westerner sees himself in relation to the universe and society. On the one hand, I knew a lot about idealism. But on the other hand, I knew nothing about it. I mean I knew a lot about idealism through the propaganda and objections of its opponent, Marxism, but I knew little about it from its own point of view. When I thought of the word "materialism"--which is a major part of Marxism and in China has repeatedly been "shown" to be the absolute truth-there were always positive connotations, and words like "right," "true," etc., flashed in my mind. On the other hand, the word "idealism" always came to me with the dark connotations that surround words like "absurd," "illogical," "wrong," etc. In China "idealism" is depicted as a ferocious and ridiculous enemy of Marxist philosophy. Idealism, as the simplified definition imprinted in my mind had it, is the view that the material world does not exist; that all that exists is the mind and its ideas. It is just the opposite of Marxist dialectical materialism which sees the mind as a product of the material world. It is not too difficult to see that idealism, with its idea that mind is of primary importance, provides a philosophical foundation for the Western emphasis on the value of individual human minds, and hence individual human beings. Therefore, my final acceptance of myself as of primary importance--an importance that overshadowed that of authority figures in English composition-was, I decided, dependent on an acceptance of idealism.

My struggle with idealism came mainly from my efforts to understand and to write about works such as Coleridge's *Literaria Biographia* and Emerson's "Over-Soul." For a long time I was frustrated and puzzled by the idealism expressed by Coleridge and Emerson-given their ideas, such as "I think, therefore I am" (Coleridge obviously borrowed from Descartes) and "the transparent eyeball" (Emerson's view of himself)-- because in my mind, drenched as it was in dialectical materialism, there was always a little voice whispering in my ear "You are, therefore you think." I could not see how human consciousness, which is not material, could create apples and trees. My intellectual conscience refused to let me believe that the human mind is the primary world and the material world secondary. Finally, I had to imagine that I was looking at a world with my head upside down. When I imagined that I was in a new body (born with the head upside down) it was easier to forget biases imprinted in my sub-consciousness about idealism, the mind, and my former self. Starting from scratch, the new inverted self-which I called my "English Self" and into which I have transformed myself--could understand and *accept*, with ease, idealism as "the truth" and "himself" (i.e., my English Self) as the "creator" of the world.

Here is how I created my new "English Self." I played a "game" similar to ones played by mental therapists. First I made a list of (simplified) features about writing associated with my old identity (the Chinese Self), both ideological and logical, and then beside the first list I added a column of features about writing associated with my new identity (the English Self). After that I pictured myself getting out of my old identity, the timid, humble, modest Chinese "I," and creeping into my new identity (often in the form of a new skin or a mask), the confident, assertive, and aggressive English "I." The new "Self" helped me to remember and accept the different rules of Chinese and English composition and the values that underpin these rules. In a sense, creating an English Self is a way of reconciling my old cultural values with the new values required by English writing, without losing the former.

An interesting structural but not material parallel to my experiences in this regard has been well described by Min-zhan Lu in her important article, "From Silence to Words: Writing as Struggle" (*College English* 49 [April 1987]: 437-48). Min-zhan Lu talks about struggles between two selves, an open self and a secret self, and between two discourses, a mainstream Marxist discourse and a bourgeois discourse her parents wanted her to learn. But her struggle was different from mine. Her Chinese self was severely constrained and suppressed by mainstream cultural discourse, but never interfused with it. Her experiences, then, were not representative of those of the majority of the younger generation who, like me, were brought up on only one discourse. I came to English composition as a Chinese person, in the fullest sense of the term, with a Chinese identity already fully formed.

Identity of the Mind: Illogical and Alogical

In learning to write in English, besides wrestling with a different ideological system, I found that I had to wrestle with a logical system very different from the blueprint of logic at the back of my mind. By "logical system" I mean two things: the Chinese way of thinking I used to approach my theme or topic in written discourse, and the Chinese critical/logical way to develop a theme or topic. By English rules, the first is illogical, for it is the opposite of the English way of approaching a topic; the second is alogical (non-logical), for it mainly uses mental pictures instead of words as a critical vehicle.

The Illogical Pattern. In English composition, an essential rule for the logical organization of a piece of writing is the use of a "topic sentence." In Chinese composition, "from surface to core" is an essential rule, a rule which means that one ought to reach a topic gradually and "systematically" instead of "abruptly."

The concept of a topic sentence, it seems to me, is symbolic of the values of a busy people in an industrialized society, rushing to get things done, hoping to attract and satisfy the busy reader very quickly. Thinking back, I realized that I did not fully understand the virtue of the concept until my life began to rush at the speed of everyone else's in this country. Chinese composition, on the other hand, seems to embody the values of a leisurely paced rural society whose inhabitants have the time to chew and taste a topic slowly. In Chinese composition, an introduction explaining how and why one chooses this topic is not only acceptable, but often regarded as necessary. It arouses the reader's interest in the topic little by little (and this is seen as a virtue of composition) and gives him/her a sense of refinement. The famous Robert B. Kaplan "noodles" contrasting a spiral Oriental thought process with a straight-line Western approach ("Cultural Thought Patterns in Inter-Cultural Education," *Readings on English as a Second Language,* Ed. Kenneth Croft, 2nd ed., Winthrop, 1980, 403-10) may be too simplistic to capture the preferred pattern of writing in English, but I think they still express some truth about Oriental writing. A Chinese writer often clears the surrounding btishes before attacking the real target. This bush-clearing pattern in Chinese writing goes back two thousand years to Kong Fuzi (Confucius). Before doing anything, Kong says in his *Luen Yu (Analects),* one first needs to call things by their proper names (expressed by his phrase "Zheng Ming" 证明.,). In other words, before touching one's main thesis, one should first state the "conditions" of composition: how, why, and when the piece is being composed. All of this will serve as a proper foundation on which to build the "house" of the piece. In the two thousand years after Kong, this principle of composition was gradually formalized (especially through the formal essays required by imperial examinations) and became known as "Ba Gu," or the eight-legged essay. The logic of Chinese composition, exemplified by the eight-legged essay, is like the peeling of an onion: layer after layer is removed until the reader finally arrives at the central point, the core.

Ba Gu still influences modern Chinese writing. Carolyn Matalene has an excellent discussion of this logical (or illogical) structure and its influence on her Chinese students' efforts to write in English ("Contrastive Rhetoric: An American Writing Teacher in China," *College English* 47 [November 19851: 789-808). A recent Chinese textbook for composition lists six essential steps (factors) for writing a narrative essay, steps to be taken in this order: time, place, character, event, cause, and consequence (*Yuwenjichu Zhishi LiushiJiang (Sixty Lessons on the Basics of the Chinese Language]*, Ed. Beijing Research Institute of Education, Beijing Publishing House, 1981, 525-609). Most Chinese students (including me) are taught to follow this sequence in composition.

The straightforward approach to composition in English seemed to me, at first, illogical. One could not jump to the topic. One had to walk step by step to reach the topic. In several of my early papers I found that the Chinese approach-the bush-clearing approach-persisted, and I had considerable difficulty writing (and in fact understanding) topic sentences. In what I deemed to be topic sentences, I grudgingly gave out themes. Today, those papers look to me like Chinese papers with forced or false English openings. For example, in a narrative paper on a trip to New York, I wrote the forced/false topic sentence, "A trip to New York in winter is boring." In the next few paragraphs, I talked about the weather, the people who went with me, and so on, before I talked about what I learned from the trip. My real thesis was that one could always learn something even on a boring trip.

The Alogical Pattern. In learning English composition, I found that there was yet another cultural blueprint affecting my logical thinking. I found from my early papers that very often I was unconsciously under the influence of a Chinese critical approach called the creation of "yijing," which is totally nonWestern. The direct translation of the word "yijing" is: yi, "mind or consciousness," and jing, "environment." An ancient approach which has existed in China for many centuries and is still the subject of much discussion, yijing is a complicated concept that defies a universal definition. But most critics in China nowadays seem to agree on one point, that yijing is the critical approach that separates Chinese literature and criticism from Western literature and criticism. Roughly speaking, yijing is the process of creating a pictorial environment while reading a piece of literature. Many critics in China believe that yijing is a creative process of inducing oneself, while reading a piece of literature or looking at a piece of art, to create mental pictures, in order to reach a unity of nature, the author, and the reader. Therefore, it is by its very nature both creative and critical. According to the theory, this nonverbal, pictorial process leads directly to a higher ground of beauty and morality. Almost all critics in China agree that yijing is not a process of logical thinking-it is not a process of moving from the premises of an argument to its conclusion, which is the foundation of Western criticism. According to yijing, the process of criticizing a piece of art or literary work has to involve the process of creation on the reader's part. In yijing, verbal thoughts and pictorial thoughts are one. Thinking is conducted largely in pictures and then "transcribed" into words. (Ezra Pound once tried to capture the creative aspect of yijing in poems such as "In a Station of the Metro." He also tried to capture the critical aspect of it in his theory of imagism and vorticism, even though he did not know the term "yijing.") One characteristic of the yijing approach to criticism, therefore, is that it often includes a description of the created mental pictures on the part of the reader/critic and his/her mental attempt to bridge (unite) the literary work, the pictures, with ultimate beauty and peace.

In looking back at my critical papers for various classes, I discovered that I unconsciously used the approach of yijing, especially in some of my earlier papers when I seemed not yet to have been in the grip of Western logical critical approaches. I wrote, for instance, an essay entitled "Wordsworth's Sound and Imagination: The Snowdon Episode." In the major part of the essay I described the pictures that flashed in my mind while I was reading passages in Wordsworth's long poem, The Prelude.

> I saw three climbers (myself among them) winding up the mountain in silence "at the dead of night," absorbed in their "private thoughts." The sky was full of blocks of clouds of different colors, freely changing their shapes, like oily pigments disturbed in a bucket of water. All of a sudden, the moonlight broke the darkness "like a flash," lighting up the mountain tops. Under the "naked moon," the band saw a vast sea of mist and vapor, a silent ocean. Then the silence was abruptly broken, and we heard the "roaring of waters, torrents, streams/Innumerable, roaring with one voice" from a "blue chasm," a fracture in the vapor of the sea. It was a joyful revelation of divine truth to the human mind: the bright, "naked" moon sheds the light of "higher reasons" and "spiritual love" upon us; the vast ocean of mist looked like a thin curtain through which we vaguely saw the infinity of nature beyond; and the sounds of roaring waters coming out of the chasm of vapor cast us into the boundless spring of imagination from the depth of the human heart. Evoked by the divine light from above, the human spring of imagination is joined by the natural spring and becomes a sustaining source of energy, feeding "upon infinity" while transcending infinity at the same time ....

Here I was describing my own experience more than Wordsworth's. The picture described by the poet is taken over and developed by the reader. The imagination of the author and the imagination of the reader are thus joined together. There was no "because" or "therefore" in the paper. There was little *logic.* And I thought it was (and it is) criticism. This seems to me a typical (but simplified) example of the yijing approach. (Incidentally, the instructor, a kind professor, found the paper interesting, though a bit "strange.")

In another paper of mine, "The Note of Life: Williams's 'The Orchestra'," I found myself describing my experiences of pictures of nature while reading William Carlos Williams's poem "The Orchestra." I "painted" these fleeting pictures and described the feelings that seemed to lead me to an understanding of a harmony, a "common tone," between man and nature. A paragraph from that paper reads:

> The poem first struck me as a musical fairy tale. With rich musical sounds in my ear, I seemed to be walking in a solitary, dense forest on a spring morning. No sound from human society could be heard. I was now sitting under a giant pine tree, ready to hear the grand concert of Nature. With the sun slowly rising from the east, the cello (the creeping creek) and the clarinet (the rustling pine trees) started with a slow overture. Enthusiastically the violinists (the twittering birds) and the French horn (the mumbling cow) "interpose[d] their voices," and the bass (bears) got in at the wrong time. The orchestra did not stop, they continued to play. The musicians of Nature do not always play in harmony. "Together, unattuned," they have to seek "a common tone" as they play along. The symphony of Nature is like the symphony of human life: both consist of random notes seeking a "common tone." For the symphony of life
>
> Love is that common tone
> shall raise his fiery head
> and sound his note.

Again, the logical pattern of this paper, the "pictorial criticism," is illogical to Western minds but "logical" to those acquainted with yijing. (Perhaps I should not even use the words "logical" and "think" because they are so conceptually tied up with "words" and with culturally-based conceptions, and therefore very misleading if not useless in a discussion of yijing. Maybe I should simply say that yijing is neither illogical nor logical, but alogical.)

I am not saying that such a pattern of "alogical" thinking is wrong-in fact some English instructors find it interesting and acceptable-but it is very non-Western. Since I was in this country to learn the English language and English literature, I had to abandon Chinese "pictorial logic," and to learn Western "verbal logic."

If I Had to Start Again

The change is profound: through my understanding of new meanings of words like "individualism," "idealism," and "I," I began to accept the underlying concepts and values of American writing, and by learning to use "topic sentences" I began to accept a new logic. Thus, when I write papers in English, I am able to obey all the general rules of English composition. In doing this I feel that I am writing through, with, and because of a new identity. I welcome the change, for it has added a new dimension to me and to my view of the world. I am not saying that I have entirely lost my Chinese identity. In fact I feel that I will never lose it. Any time I write in Chinese, I resume my old identity, and obey the rules of Chinese composition such as "Make the 'I' modest," and "Beat around the bush before attacking the central topic." It is necessary for me to have such a Chinese identity in order to write authentic Chinese. (I have seen people who, after learning to write in English, use English logic and sentence patterning to write Chinese. They produce very awkward Chinese texts.) But when I write in English, I imagine myself slipping into a new "skin," and I let the "I" behave much more aggressively and knock the topic right on the head. Being conscious of these different identities has helped me to reconcile different systems of values and logic, and has played a pivotal role in my learning to compose in English. 466 College Composition and Communication 40 (December 1989)

Looking back, I realize that the process of learning to write in English is in fact a process of creating and defining a new identity and balancing it with the old identity. The process of learning English composition would have been easier if I had realized this earlier and consciously sought to compare the two different identities required by the two writing systems from two different cultures. It is fine and perhaps even necessary for American composition teachers to teach about topic sentences, paragraphs, the use of punctuation, documentation, and so on, but can anyone design exercises sensitive to the ideological and logical differences that students like me experience-and design them so they can be introduced at an early stage of an English composition class? As I pointed out earlier, the traditional advice "Just be yourself" is not clear and helpful to students from Korea, China, Vietnam, or India. From "Be yourself" we are likely to hear either "Forget your cultural habit of writing" or "Write as you would write in your own language." But neither of the two is what the instructor meant or what we want to do. It would be helpful if he or she pointed out the different cultural/ideological connotations of the word "I," the connotations that exist in a group-centered culture and an individual-centered culture. To sharpen the contrast, it might be useful to design papers on topics like "The Individual vs. The Group: China vs. America" or "Different 'I's' in Different Cultures."

Carolyn Matalene mentioned in her article (789) an incident concerning American businessmen who presented their Chinese hosts with gifts of cheddar cheese, not knowing that the Chinese generally do not like cheese. Liking cheddar cheese may not be essential to writing English prose, but being truly accustomed to the social norms that stand behind ideas such as the English "I" and the logical pattern of English composition-call it "compositional cheddar cheese"-is essential to writing in English. Matalene does not provide an "elixir" to help her Chinese students like English "compositional cheese," but rather recommends, as do I, that composition teachers not be afraid to give foreign students English "cheese," but to make sure to hand it out slowly, sympathetically, and fully realizing that it tastes very peculiar in the mouths of those used to a very different cuisine.

If Black English Isn't a Language, Then Tell Me, What Is?

James Baldwin

James Baldwin (1924–1987) was born in poverty in the Harlem district of New York City, where he lived until he was eighteen. From age fourteen to seventeen he was a revivalist minister, manifesting a religious intensity seen in much of his work. After high school he worked various jobs in Greenwich Village while studying and writing on his own. He then moved to Paris for eight years, and thereafter much of his life was spent back and forth between New York and Europe. In the early 1960s Baldwin worked in the civil rights movement and had already written and published several successful novels. He continued writing up until his death in France. His novels include Go Tell It on the Mountain *(1953),* Giovanni's Room *(1956), and* Another Country *(1967). His best-known collections of essays are* Notes of a Native Son *(1955),* Nobody Knows My Name *(1961), and* The Fire Next Time. *His play* Blues for Mister Charley *(1964) is equally powerful. In the following essay written for* The New York Times *in 1979, Baldwin analyzes what it means to be a language and how black English evolved to fulfill an important role for black Americans. Although he does not discuss at length the practical question of what it means to accept black English in the schools, his larger argument for the existence and importance of black English as a separate language has clear implications for the American educational system.*

---

1 The argument concerning the use, or the status, or the reality, 1
of black English is rooted in American history and has absolutely nothing to do with the question the argument supposes itself to be posing. The argument has nothing to do with language itself but with the role of language. Language, incontestably, reveals the speaker. Language, also, far more dubiously, is meant to define the other—and, in this case, the other is refusing to be defined by a language that has never been able to recognize him.

People evolve a language in order to describe and thus control their circumstances, or in order not to be submerged by a situation that they cannot articulate. (And if they cannot articulate it, they *are* submerged.) A Frenchman living in Paris speaks a subtly and crucially different language from that of the man living in Marseilles; neither sounds very much like a man living in Quebec; and they would all have great difficulty in apprehending what the man from Guadeloupe, or Martinique, is saying, to say nothing of the man from Senegal—although the "common" language of all these areas is French. But each has paid, and is paying, a different price for this "common" language, in which, as it turns out, they are not saying, and cannot be saying, the same things: They each have very different realities to articulate, or control.

What joins all languages, and all men, is the necessity to confront life, in order, not inconceivably, to outwit death: The price for this is the acceptance, and achievement, of one's temporal identity. So that, for example, though it is not taught in the schools (and this has the potential of becoming a political issue) the south of France still clings to its ancient and musical Provençal, which resists being described as a "dialect." And much of the tension in the Basque countries, and in Wales, is due to the Basque and Welsh determination not to allow their languages to be destroyed. This determination also feeds the flames in Ireland for among the many indignities the Irish have been forced to undergo at English hands is the English contempt for their language.

It goes without saying, then, that language is also a political instrument, means, and proof of power. It is the most vivid and crucial key to identity. It reveals the private identity, and connects one with, or divorces one from, the larger, public, or communal identity. There have been, and are, times, and places, when to speak a certain language could be dangerous, even fatal. Or, one may speak the same language, but in such a way that one's antecedents are revealed, or (one hopes) hidden. This is true in France, and is absolutely true in England: The range (and reign) of accents on that damp little island make England coherent for the English and totally incomprehensible for everyone else. To open your mouth in England is (if I may use black English) to "put your business in the street": You have confessed your parents, your youth, your school, your salary, your self-esteem, and, alas, your future.

5 Now, I do not know what white Americans would sound like if there had never been any black people in the United States, but they would not sound the way they sound. *Jazz,* for example, is a very specific sexual term, as in *jazz me, baby,* but white people purified it into the Jazz Age. *Sock it to me,* which means, roughly, the same thing, has been adopted by Nathaniel Hawthorne's descendants with no qualms or hesitations at all, along with *let it all hang out* and *right on! Beat to his socks,* which was once the black's most total and despairing image of poverty, was transformed into a thing called the Beat Generation, which phenomenon was, largely, composed of *uptight,* middle-class white people, imitating poverty, trying to *get down,* to get *with it,* doing their *thing,* doing their despairing best to be *funky,* which we, the blacks, never dreamed of doing—we *were* funky, baby, like *funk* was going out of style.

Now, no one can eat his cake, and have it, too, and it is late in the day to attempt to penalize black people for having created a language that permits the nation its only glimpse of reality, a language without which the nation would be even more *whipped* than it is.

I say that the present skirmish is rooted in American history, and it is. Black English is the creation of the black diaspora. Blacks came to the United States chained to each other, but from different tribes. Neither could speak the other's language. If two black people, at that bitter hour of the world's history, had been able to speak to each other, the institution of chattel slavery could never have lasted as long as it did. Subsequently, the slave was given, under the eye, and the gun, of his master, Congo Square, and the Bible—or, in other words, and under those conditions, the slave began the formation of the black church, and it is within this unprecedented tabernacle that black English began to be formed. This was not, merely, as in the European example, the adoption of a foreign tongue, but an alchemy that transformed ancient elements into a new language: *A language comes into existence by means of brutal necessity, and the rules of the language are dictated by what the language must convey.*

There was a moment, in time, and in this place, when my brother, or my mother, or my father, or my sister, had to convey to me, for example, the danger in which I was standing from the white man standing just behind me, and to convey this with a speed and in a language, that the white man could not possibly understand, and that, indeed, he cannot understand, until today. He cannot afford to understand it. This understanding would reveal to him too much about himself and smash that mirror before which he has been frozen for so long.

Now, if this passion, this skill, this (to quote Toni Morrison) "sheer intelligence," this incredible music, the mighty achievement of having brought a people utterly unknown to, or despised by "history"—to have brought this people to their present, troubled, troubling, and unassailable and unanswerable place—if this absolutely unprecedented journey does not indicate that black English is a language, I am curious to know what definition of languages is to be trusted.

10 A people at the center of the western world, and in the midst of 10 so hostile a population, has not endured and transcended by means of what is patronizingly called a "dialect." We, the blacks, are in trouble, certainly, but we are not inarticulate because we are not compelled to defend a morality that we know to be a lie.

The brutal truth is that the bulk of the white people in America never had any interest in educating black people, except as this could serve white purposes. It is not the black child's language that is despised. It is his experience. A child cannot be taught by anyone who despises him, and a child cannot afford to be fooled. A child cannot be taught by anyone whose demand, essentially, is that the child repudiate his experience, and all that gives him sustenance, and enter a limbo in which he will no longer be black, and in which he knows that he can never become white. Black people have lost too many black children that way.

And, after all, finally, in a country with standards so untrustworthy, a country that makes heroes of so many criminal mediocrities, a country unable to face why so many of the nonwhite are in prison, or on the needle, or standing, futureless, in the streets—it may very well be that both the child, and his elder, have concluded that they have nothing whatever to learn from the people of a country that has managed to learn so little.

How to Tame a Wild Tongue

Gloria Anzaldúa

Gloria Anzaldúa (1942–2004), a Mexican-American feminist writer, grew up in southwest Texas. The author of Borderlands/La Frontera: The New Mestiza *(1987), she also edited two volumes of minority women's writing,* This Bridge Called My Back: Writing by Radical Women of Color *(1983) and* Hacienda Caras: Making Face/Making Soul *(1990). Anzaldúa also wrote two children's books,* Friends from the Other Side/Amigos del Otro Lado *(1993) and* Prietita and the Ghost Woman/Prietita y la Llorona *(1995), in addition to a memoir-like collection of interviews titled* Interviews/Ientrevistas *(2000). In this essay, a chapter from* Borderlands, *Anzaldúa describes the history and vital importance of her language and its many variations.*

1 "We're going to have to control your tongue," the dentist says, pulling out all the metal from my mouth. Silver bits plop and tinkle into the basin. My mouth is a motherlode. 1

The dentist is cleaning out my roots. I get a whiff of the stench when I gasp. "I can't cap that tooth yet, you're still draining," he says.

"We're going to have to do something about your tongue," I hear the anger rising in his voice. My tongue keeps pushing out the wads of cotton, pushing back the drills, the long thin needles. "I've never seen anything as strong or as stubborn," he says. And I think, how do you tame a wild tongue, train it to be quiet, how do you bridle and saddle it? How do you make it lie down?

"Who is to say that robbing a people of
its language is less violent than war?"

—Ray Gwyn Smith[1]

I remember being caught speaking Spanish at recess—that was good for three licks on the knuckles with a sharp ruler. I remember being sent to the corner of the classroom for "talking back" to the Anglo teacher when all I was trying to do was tell her how to pronounce my name. "If you want to be American, speak 'American.' If you don't like it, go back to Mexico where you belong."

5 "I want you to speak English. *Pa' hallar buen trabajo tienes que saber hablar el inglés bien. Qué vale toda tu educación si todavía hables inglés con un 'accent,'* " my mother would say, mortified that I spoke English like a Mexican. At Pan American University, I, and all Chicano students, were required to take two speech classes. Their purpose: to get rid of our accents.

Attacks on one's form of expression with the intent to censor are a violation of the First Amendment. *El Anglo con cara de inocente nos arrancó la lengua.* Wild tongues can't be tamed, they can only be cut out.

Overcoming the Tradition of Silence

Ahogadas, escupimos el oscuro.
Peleando con nuestra propia sombra
el silencio nos sepulta.

En boca cerrada no entran moscas. "Flies don't enter a closed mouth" is a saying I kept hearing when I was a child. *Ser habladora* was to be a gossip and a liar, to talk too much. *Muchachitas bien criadas,* well-bred girls, don't answer back. *Es una falta de respeto* to talk back to one's mother or father. I remember one of the sins I'd recite to the priest in the confession box the few times I went to confession: talking back to my mother, *hablar pa' 'tras, replar. Hocicona, repelona, chismosa,* having a big mouth, questioning, carrying tales are all signs of being *mal criada.* In my culture they are all words that are derogatory if applied to women—I've never heard them applied to men.

[1]Ray Gwyn Smith, *Moorland Is Cold Country,* unpublished book.

The first time I heard two women, a Puerto Rican and a Cuban, say the word "*nosotras,*" I was shocked. I had not known the word existed. Chicanos use *nosotros* whether we're male or female. We are robbed of our female being by the masculine plural. Language is a male discourse.

And our tongues have become
dry   the wilderness has
dried out our tongues   and
we have forgotten speech.
—Irena Klepfisz[2]

Even our own people, other Spanish speakers *nos quieren poner candados en la boca.* They would hold us back with their bag of *reglas de academia.*

Oyé como ladra: el lenguaje de la frontera

Quien tiene boca se equivoca.
—Mexican saying

"*Pocho,* cultural traitor, you're speaking the oppressor's language by speaking English, you're ruining the Spanish language," I have been accused by various Latinos and Latinas. Chicano Spanish is considered by the purist and by most Latinos deficient, a mutilation of Spanish.

But Chicano Spanish is a border tongue which developed naturally. Change, *evolución, enriquecimiento de palabras nuevas por invención o adopción* have created variants of Chicano Spanish, *un nuevo lenguaje. Un lenguaje que corresponde a un modo de vivir.* Chicano Spanish is not incorrect; it is a living language.

For a people who are neither Spanish nor live in a country in which Spanish is the first language; for a people who live in a country in which English is the reigning tongue but who are not Anglo; for a people who cannot identify with either standard (formal, Castilian) Spanish nor standard English, what recourse is left to them but to create their own

[2]Irena Klepfisz, "*Di rayze aheym*/The Journey Home," in *The Tribe of Dina: A Jewish Women's Anthology,* Melanie Kaye/Kantrowitz and Irena Klepfisz, eds. (Montpelier, VT: Sinister Wisdom Books, 1986), 49.

language? A language which they can connect their identity to, one capable of communicating the realities and values true to themselves—a language with terms that are neither *español ni inglés,* but both. We speak a *patois,* a forked tongue, a variation of two languages.

Chicano Spanish sprang out of the Chicanos' need to identify ourselves as a distinct people. We needed a language with which we could communicate with ourselves, a secret language. For some of us, language is a homeland closer than the Southwest—for many Chicanos today live in the Midwest and the East. And because we are a complex, heterogeneous people, we speak many languages. Some of the languages we speak are:

1. Standard English
2. Working class and slang English
3. Standard Spanish
4. Standard Mexican Spanish
5. North Mexican Spanish dialect
6. Chicano Spanish (Texas, New Mexico, Arizona and California have regional variations)
7. Tex-Mex
8. *Pachuco* (called *caló*)

My "home" tongues are the languages I speak with my sister and brothers, with my friends. They are the last five listed, with 6 and 7 being closest to my heart. From school, the media and job situations, I've picked up standard and working class English. From Mamagrande Locha and from reading Spanish and Mexican literature, I've picked up Standard Spanish and Standard Mexican Spanish. From *los recién llegados,* Mexican immigrants, and *braceros,* I learned the North Mexican dialect. With Mexicans I'll try to speak either Standard Mexican Spanish or the North Mexican dialect. From my parents and Chicanos living in the Valley, I picked up Chicano Texas Spanish, and I speak it with my mom, younger brother (who married a Mexican and who rarely mixes Spanish with English), and aunts and older relatives.

15 With Chicanas from *Nuevo México* or *Arizona* I will speak Chicano Spanish a little, but often they don't understand what I'm saying. With most California Chicanas I speak entirely in English (unless I forget). When I first moved to San Francisco, I'd rattle off something in Spanish, unintentionally embarrassing them. Often it is only with another Chicana *tejana* that I can talk freely.

Words distorted by English are known as anglicisms or *pochismos.* The *pocho* is an anglicized Mexican or American of Mexican origin who speaks Spanish with an accent characteristic of North Americans and who distorts and reconstructs the language according to the influence of English.[3] Tex-Mex, or Spanglish, comes most naturally to me. I may switch back and forth from English to Spanish in the same sentence or in the same word. With my sister and my brother Nune and with Chicano *tejano* contemporaries I speak in Tex-Mex.

From kids and people my own age I picked up *Pachuco. Pachuco* (the language of the zoot suiters) is a language of rebellion, both against Standard Spanish and Standard English. It is a secret language. Adults of the culture and outsiders cannot understand it. It is made up of slang words from both English and Spanish. *Ruca* means girl or woman, *vato* means guy or dude, *chale* means no, *simón* means yes, *churro* is sure, talk is *periquiar, pigionear* means petting, *qué gacho* means how nerdy, *ponte áquila* means watch out, death is called *la pelona.* Through lack of practice and not having others who can speak it, I've lost most of the *Pachuco* tongue.

Chicano Spanish

Chicanos, after 250 years of Spanish/Anglo colonization, have developed significant differences in the Spanish we speak. We collapse two adjacent vowels into a single syllable and sometimes shift the stress in certain words such as *maíz/maiz, cohete/cuete.* We leave out certain consonants when they appear between vowels: *lado/lao, mojado/mojao.* Chicanos from South Texas pronounce *f* as *j* as in *jue (fue).* Chicanos use "archaisms," words that are no longer in the Spanish language, words that have been evolved out. We say *semos, truje, haiga, ansina,* and *naiden.* We retain the "archaic" *j,* as in *jalar,* that derives from an earlier *h,* (the French *halar* or the Germanic *halon* which was lost to standard Spanish in the 16th century), but which is still found in several regional dialects such as the one spoken in South Texas. (Due to geography, Chicanos from the Valley of South Texas were cut off linguistically from other Spanish speakers. We tend to use words that the Spaniards brought over from Medieval Spain. The majority of the

[3] R. C. Ortega, *Dialectología Del Barrio,* trans. Hortencia S. Alwan (Los Angeles, CA: R. C. Ortega Publisher & Bookseller, 1977), 132.

Spanish colonizers in Mexico and the Southwest came from Extremadura—Hernán Cortés was one of them—and Andalucía. Andalucians pronounce *ll* like a *y,* and their *d*'s tend to be absorbed by adjacent vowels: *tirado* becomes *tirao.* They brought *el lenguaje popular, dialectos y regionalismos.*[4])

Chicanos and other Spanish speakers also shift *ll* to *y* and *z* to *s.*[5] We leave out initial syllables, saying *tar* for *estar, toy* for *estoy, hora* for *ahora* (*cubanos* and *puertorriqueños* also leave out initial letters of some words.) We also leave out the final syllable such as *pa* for *para.* The intervocalic *y,* the *ll* as in *tortilla, ella, botella,* gets replaced by *tortia* or *tortiya, ea, botea.* We add an additional syllable at the beginning of certain words: *atocar* for *tocar, agastar* for *gastar.* Sometimes we'll say *lavaste las vacijas,* other times *lavates* (substituting the *ates* verb endings for the *aste*).

20 We use anglicisms, words borrowed from English: *bola* from ball, *carpeta* from carpet, *máchina de lavar* (instead of *lavadora*) from washing machine. Tex-Mex argot, created by adding a Spanish sound at the beginning or end of an English word such as *cookiar* for cook, *watchiar* for watch, *parkiar* for park, and *rapiar* for rape, is the result of the pressures on Spanish speakers to adapt to English.

We don't use the word *vosotros/as* or its accompanying verb form. We don't say *claro* (to mean yes), *imagínate,* or *me emociona,* unless we picked up Spanish from Latinas, out of a book, or in a classroom. Other Spanish-speaking groups are going through the same, or similar, development in their Spanish.

Linguistic Terrorism

> *Deslenguadas. Somos los del español deficiente.* We are your linguistic nightmare, your linguistic aberration, your linguistic *mestisaje,* the subject of your *burla.* Because we speak with tongues of fire we are culturally crucified. Racially, culturally and linguistically *somos huérfanos*—we speak an orphan tongue.

Chicanas who grew up speaking Chicano Spanish have internalized the belief that we speak poor Spanish. It is illegitimate, a bastard

---

[4]Eduardo Hernández-Chávez, Andrew D. Cohen, and Anthony F. Beltramo, *El Lenguaje de los Chicanos: Regional and Social Characteristics Used By Mexican Americans* (Arlington, VA: Center for Applied Linguistics, 1975), 39.

[5]Hernández-Chávez, xvii.

language. And because we internalize how our language has been used against us by the dominant culture, we use our language differences against each other.

Chicana feminists often skirt around each other with suspicion and hesitation. For the longest time I couldn't figure it out. Then it dawned on me. To be close to another Chicana is like looking into the mirror. We are afraid of what we'll see there. *Pena.* Shame. Low estimation of self. In childhood we are told that our language is wrong. Repeated attacks on our native tongue diminish our sense of self. The attacks continue throughout our lives.

Chicanas feel uncomfortable talking in Spanish to Latinas, afraid of their censure. Their language was not outlawed in their countries. They had a whole lifetime of being immersed in their native tongue; generations, centuries in which Spanish was a first language, taught in school, heard on radio and TV, and read in the newspaper.

If a person, Chicana or Latina, has a low estimation of my native tongue, she also has a low estimation of me. Often with *mexicanas y latinas* we'll speak English as a neutral language. Even among Chicanas we tend to speak English at parties or conferences. Yet, at the same time, we're afraid the other will think we're *agringadas* because we don't speak Chicano Spanish. We oppress each other trying to out-Chicano each other, vying to be the "real" Chicanas, to speak like Chicanos. There is no one Chicano language just as there is no one Chicano experience. A monolingual Chicana whose first language is English or Spanish is just as much a Chicana as one who speaks several variants of Spanish. A Chicana from Michigan or Chicago or Detroit is just as much a Chicana as one from the Southwest. Chicano Spanish is as diverse linguistically as it is regionally.

By the end of this century, Spanish speakers will comprise the biggest minority group in the U.S., a country where students in high schools and colleges are encouraged to take French classes because French is considered more "cultured." But for a language to remain alive it must be used.[6] By the end of this century English, and not Spanish, will be the mother tongue of most Chicanos and Latinos.

So, if you want to really hurt me, talk badly about my language. Ethnic identity is twin skin to linguistic identity—I am my language.

---

[6] Irena Klepfisz, "Secular Jewish Identity: Yidishkayt in American," in *The Tribe of Dina,* Kaye/Kantrowitz and Klepfisz, eds., 43.

Until I can take pride in my language, I cannot take pride in myself. Until I can accept as legitimate Chicano Texas Spanish, Tex-Mex and all the other languages I speak, I cannot accept the legitimacy of myself. Until I am free to write bilingually and to switch codes without having always to translate, while I still have to speak English or Spanish when I would rather speak Spanglish, and as long as I have to accommodate the English speakers rather than having them accommodate me, my tongue will be illegitimate.

I will no longer be made to feel ashamed of existing. I will have my voice: Indian, Spanish, white. I will have my serpent's tongue—my woman's voice, my sexual voice, my poet's voice. I will overcome the tradition of silence.

> My fingers
> move sly against your palm
> Like women everywhere, we speak in code. . . .
>
> —Melanie Kaye/Kantrowitz[7]

"Vistas," corridos, y comida: My Native Tongue

In the 1960s, I read my first Chicano novel. It was *City of Night* by John Rechy, a gay Texan, son of a Scottish father and a Mexican mother. For days I walked around in stunned amazement that a Chicano could write and could get published. When I read *I Am Joaquín*[8] I was surprised to see a bilingual book by a Chicano in print. When I saw poetry written in Tex-Mex for the first time, a feeling of pure joy flashed through me. I felt like we really existed as a people. In 1971, when I started teaching High School English to Chicano students, I tried to supplement required texts with works by Chicanos, only to be reprimanded and forbidden to do so by the principal. He claimed that I was supposed to teach "American" and English literature. At the risk of being fired, I swore my students to secrecy and slipped in Chicano short stories, poems, a play. In graduate school, while working toward a Ph.D., I had to "argue" with one advisor after the other, semester

---

[7]Melanie Kaye/Kantrowitz, "Sign," in *We Speak in Code: Poems and other Writings* (Pittsburgh, PA: Motheroot Publications, Inc., 1980), 85.

[8]Rodolfo Gonzales, *I Am Joaquín/Yo Soy Joaquín* (New York, NY: Bantam Books, 1972). It was first published in 1967.

after semester, before I was allowed to make Chicano literature an area of focus.

30 Even before I read books by Chicanos or Mexicans, it was the 30
Mexican movies I saw at the drive-in—the Thursday night specials of $1.00 a carload—that gave me a sense of belonging. "*Vámonos a las vistas,*" my mother would call out and we'd all—grandmother, brothers, sister and cousins—squeeze into the car. We'd wolf down cheese and bologna white bread sandwiches while watching Pedro Infante in melodramatic tearjerkers like *Nosotros los pobres,* the first "real" Mexican movie (that was not an imitation of European movies). I remember seeing *Cuando los hijos se van* and surmising that all Mexican movies played up the love a mother has for her children and what ungrateful sons and daughters suffer when they are not devoted to their mothers. I remember the singing-type "westerns" of Jorge Negrete and Miquel Aceves Mejía. When watching Mexican movies, I felt a sense of homecoming as well as alienation. People who were to amount to something didn't go to Mexican movies, or *bailes* or tune their radios to *bolero, rancherita,* and *corrido* music.

The whole time I was growing up, there was *norteño* music, sometimes called North Mexican border music, or Tex-Mex music, or Chicano music, or *cantina* (bar) music. I grew up listening to *conjuntos,* three- or four-piece bands made up of folk musicians playing guitar, *baja sexto,* drums and button accordion, which Chicanos had borrowed from the German immigrants who had come to Central Texas and Mexico to farm and build breweries. In the Rio Grande Valley, Steve Jordan and Little Joe Hernández were popular, and Flaco Jiménez was the accordion king. The rhythms of Tex-Mex music are those of the polka, also adapted from the Germans, who in turn had borrowed the polka from the Czechs and Bohemians.

I remember the hot, sultry evenings when *corridos*—songs of love and death on the Texas-Mexican borderlands—reverberated out of cheap amplifiers from the local *cantinas* and wafted in through my bedroom window.

Corridos first became widely used along the South Texas/Mexican border during the early conflict between Chicanos and Anglos. The *corridos* are usually about Mexican heroes who do valiant deeds against the Anglo oppressors. Pancho Villa's song, *"La cucaracha,"* is the most famous one. *Corridos* of John F. Kennedy and his death are still very popular in the Valley. Older Chicanos remember Lydia Mendoza, one of the great border corrido singers who was called *la Gloria de Tejas.* Her *"El tango negro,"* sung during the Great Depression, made her a singer of the people. The ever present *corridos* narrated one hundred years of border history, bringing news of events as well as entertaining. These folk musicians and folk songs are our chief cultural mythmakers, and they made our hard lives seem bearable.

I grew up feeling ambivalent about our music. Country-western and rock-and-roll had more status. In the 50s and 60s, for the slightly educated and *agringado* Chicanos, there existed a sense of shame at being caught listening to our music. Yet I couldn't stop my feet from thumping to the music, could not stop humming the words, nor hide from myself the exhilaration I felt when I heard it.

35 There are more subtle ways that we internalize identification, especially in the forms of images and emotions. For me food and certain smells are tied to my identity, to my homeland. Woodsmoke curling up to an immense blue sky; woodsmoke perfuming my grandmother's clothes, her skin. The stench of cow manure and the yellow patches on the ground; the crack of a .22 rifle and the reek of cordite. Homemade white cheese sizzling in a pan, melting inside a folded *tortilla.* My sister Hilda's hot, spicy *menudo, chile colorado* making it deep red, pieces of *panza* and hominy floating on top. My brother Carito barbecuing *fajitas* in the backyard. Even now and 3,000 miles away, I can see my mother spicing the ground beef, pork and venison with *chile.* My mouth salivates at the thought of the hot steaming *tamales* I would be eating if I were home.

Si le preguntas a mi mamá, "¿Qué eres?"

> Identity is the essential core of who
> we are as individuals, the conscious
> experience of the self inside.
>
> —Kaufman[9]

Nosotros los chicanos straddle the borderlands. On one side of us, we are constantly exposed to the Spanish of the Mexicans, on the other side we hear the Anglos' incessant clamoring so that we forget our language. Among ourselves we don't say *nosotros los americanos, o nosotros*

[9]Kaufman, 68.

los españoles, o nosotros los hispanos. We say *nosotros los mexicanos* (by *mexicanos* we do not mean citizens of Mexico; we do not mean a national identity, but a racial one). We distinguish between *mexicanos del otro lado* and *mexicanos de este lado.* Deep in our hearts we believe that being Mexican has nothing to do with which country one lives in. Being Mexican is a state of soul—not one of mind, not one of citizenship. Neither eagle nor serpent, but both. And like the ocean, neither animal respects borders.

> *Dime con quien andas y te diré quien eres.*
> (Tell me who your friends are and I'll tell you who you are.)
>
> —Mexican saying

Si le preguntas a mi mamá, "¿Qué eres?" te dirá. "Soy mexicana." My brothers and sisters say the same. I sometimes will answer *"soy mexicana"* and at others will say *"soy chicana" o "soy tejana."* But I identified as *"Raza"* before I ever identified as *"mexicana"* or *"chicana"*.

As a culture, we call ourselves Spanish when referring to ourselves as a linguistic group and when copping out. It is then that we forget our predominant Indian genes. We are 70–80% Indian.[10] We call ourselves Hispanic[11] or Spanish-American or Latin-American or Latin when linking ourselves to other Spanish-speaking peoples of the Western hemisphere and when copping out. We call ourselves Mexican-American[12] to signify we are neither Mexican nor American, but more the noun "American" than the adjective "Mexican" (and when copping out).

Chicanos and other people of color suffer economically for not acculturating. This voluntary (yet forced) alienation makes for psychological conflict, a kind of dual identity—we don't identify with the Anglo-American cultural values and we don't totally identify with the Mexican cultural values. We are a synergy of the two cultures with various degrees of Mexicanness or Angloness. I have so internalized the borderland conflict that sometimes I feel like one cancels out the

---

[10]Hernández-Chávez, 88–90.

[11]"Hispanic" is derived from *Hispania* (*España*), a name given to the Iberian Peninsula in ancient times when it was part of the Roman Empire, and is a term designated by the U.S. government to make it easier to handle us on paper.

[12]The Treaty of Guadalupe Hidalgo created the Mexican-American in 1848.

other and we are zero, nothing, no one. *A veces no soy nada ni nadie. Pero hasta cuando no lo soy, lo soy.*

40 When not copping out, when we know we are more than nothing, we call ourselves Mexican, referring to race and ancestry; *mestizo* when affirming both our Indian and Spanish (but we hardly ever own our Black ancestry); Chicano when referring to a politically aware people born and/or raised in the U.S.; *Raza* when referring to Chicanos; *tejanos* when we are Chicanos from Texas. 40

Chicanos did not know we were a people until 1965 when César Chávez and the farmworkers united and *I Am Joaquín* was published and *la Raza Unida* party was formed in Texas. With that recognition, we became a distinct people. Something momentous happened to the Chicano soul—we became aware of our reality and acquired a name and a language (Chicano Spanish) that reflected that reality. Now that we had a name, some of the fragmented pieces began to fall together—who we were, what we were, how we had evolved. We began to get glimpses of what we might eventually become.

Yet the struggle of identities continues, the struggle of borders is our reality still. One day the inner struggle will cease and a true integration take place. In the meantime, *tenemos que hacer la lucha. ¿Quién está protegiendo los ranchos de mi gente? ¿Quién está tratando de cerrar la fisura entre la india y el blanco en nuestra sangre? El chicano, si, el chicano que anda como un ladrón en su propia casa.*

Los chicanos, how patient we seem, how very patient. There is the quiet of the Indian about us.[13] We know how to survive. When other races have given up their tongue, we've kept ours. We know what it is to live under the hammer blow of the dominant *norteamericano* culture. But more than we count the blows, we count the days the weeks the years the centuries the eons until the white laws and commerce and customs will rot in the deserts they've created, lie bleached. *Humildes* yet proud, *quietos* yet wild, *nosotros los mexicanos-chicanos* will walk by the crumbling ashes as we go about our business. Stubborn, persevering, impenetrable as stone, yet possessing a malleability that renders us unbreakable, we, the *mestizas* and *mestizos,* will remain.

---

[13]Anglos, in order to alleviate their guilt for dispossessing the Chicano, stressed the Spanish part of us and perpetuated the myth of the Spanish Southwest. We have accepted the fiction that we are Hispanic, that is Spanish, in order to accommodate ourselves to the dominant culture and its abhorrence of Indians. Hernández-Chávez, 88–91.

Additional Credit Lines

- "The Uses of Sidewalks: Safety," by Jane Jacobs, reprinted from *The Death and Life of Great American Cities* (1961), by permission of Vintage Books, a division of Random House, Inc.
- "Immigration Myths and Facts," reprinted by permission from *American Civil Liberties Union*, January 2008, www.aclu.org.
- "The North American," by Richard Rodriguez, reprinted from *Public Discourse in America: Conversation and Community in the 21st Century*, edited by Judith Rodin and Stephan Steinberg (2003), by permission of the University of Pennsylvania Press.
- "The Classroom and the Wider Culture: Identity as a Key to Learning English Composition," by Fan Shen, reprinted from *College Composition and Communication* (1989), by permission of the National Council of Teachers of English.
- "We Are All Works in Progress," by Leslie Feinberg, reprinted from *Trans Liberation: Beyond Pink and Blue* (1998), by permission of Beacon Press.